COLLINS LIVING HISTORY

The Italian Renaissance

Fiona Macdonald
Series editor: Christopher Culpin

CollinsEducational
An imprint of HarperCollinsPublishers

Contents

UNIT 1 A divided land — page 6
UNIT 2 Princes and patrons — 16
UNIT 3 A rebirth of art — 28
UNIT 4 Renaissance heritage — 50
Glossary and pronunciation guide — 60
Index — 63

attainment target 1

Questions aimed at this attainment target find out how much you know and understand about the past. Some questions are about how things were different in history: not only people's food or clothes, but their beliefs too. Others are about how things change through history, sometimes quickly, sometimes slowly, sometimes a little, sometimes a lot. Other questions ask you to explain why things were different in the past, and why changes took place.

attainment target 2

This attainment target is about understanding what people say about the past. Historians, as well as lots of other people, try to describe what the past was like. Sometimes they say different things. This attainment target is about understanding these differences and why they occur.

attainment target 3

This attainment target is about historical sources and how we use them to find out about the past. Some questions are about the historical evidence we can get from sources. Others ask you about how valuable this evidence might be.

Introduction

This book is about the civilisation of the RENAISSANCE in Italy. It looks at the way in which new ideas and attitudes that flourished there gradually spread throughout Europe, and across the world. You will see that, in several ways, the achievements of Renaissance Italy still influence our lives today.

What was the Renaissance? The word itself simply means 're-birth'. Historians use it to describe what happened during a period of about 150 years, from around AD 1400 to 1550. During those years, there was a remarkable increase in artistic output of all kinds. New and revolutionary styles appeared, in buildings like the cathedral in Florence (shown below), paintings, sculptures, metalwork, furniture and jewellery. As well as these artistic changes, there was also a revolution in the world of learning. SCHOLARS rediscovered ancient Greek and Roman ideas, and used them to criticise the MEDIEVAL, Christian attitudes and beliefs they had been taught. They developed a new PHILOSOPHY, known as HUMANISM, and a more modern, questioning, scientific outlook on the world. All of these Renaissance ideas spread rapidly thanks to the invention of printing, and to the generosity of PATRONS, who supported artists and scholars while they worked.

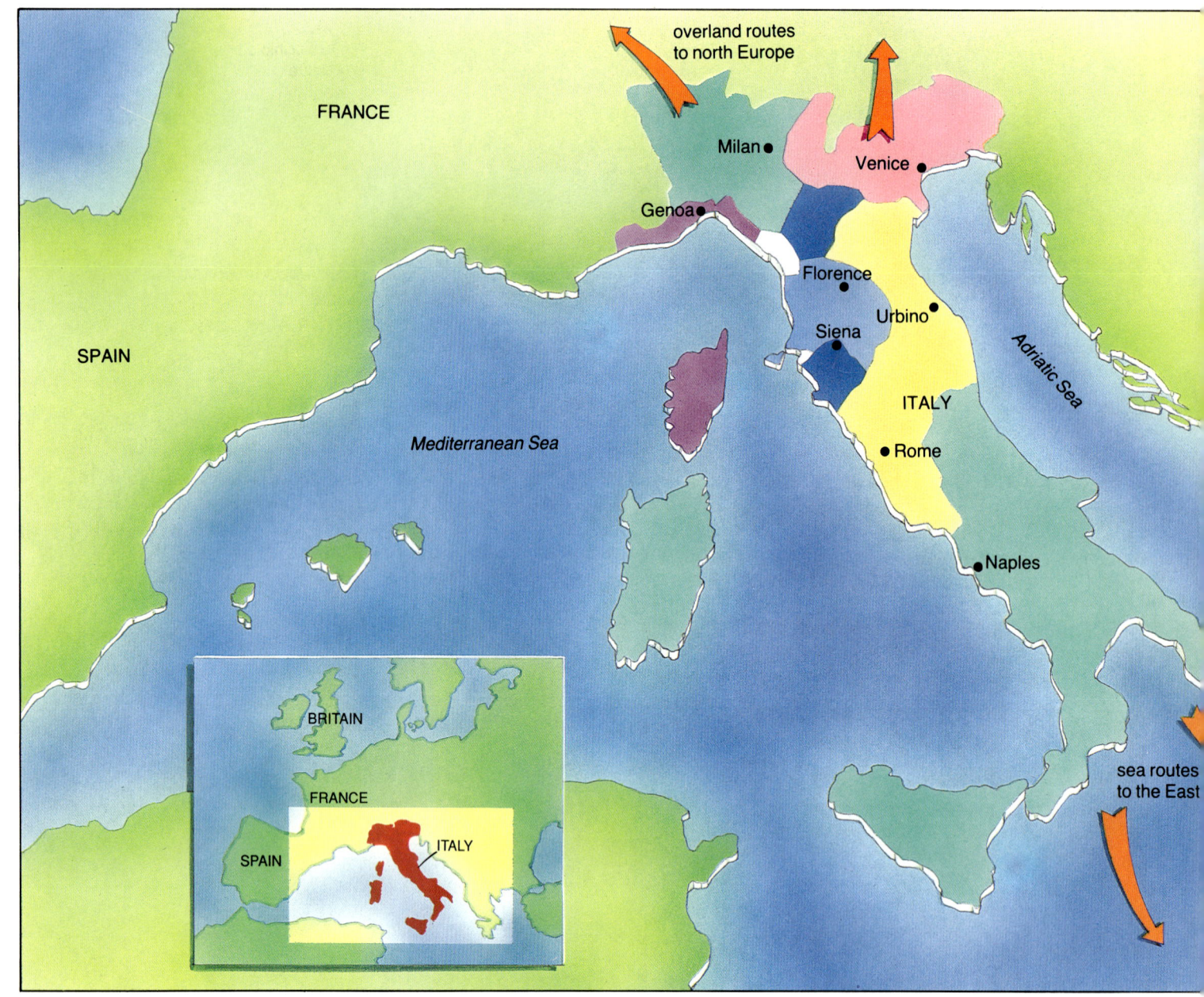

Italy in the 15th century, showing the more important city-states.

This book will introduce you to some typical Renaissance ideas and designs. You may, or may not, like the buildings and works of art produced in Renaissance times. You may, or may not, share Renaissance scholars' enthusiasm for Greek and Roman remains, or their interest in exploration and scientific discovery. You may think that humanism is a sensible or a silly philosophy. But as you read through this book and study the Sources, you will be finding out more about a group of daring, energetic, creative and thoughtful people who lived over 400 years ago.

By looking at the timeline opposite, you can discover some of the major events in the history of the Italian Renaissance, from its earliest beginnings to its eventual decline. You can trace how Renaissance ideas spread from their Italian birthplace through Europe to other, distant lands.

KEY
Naples
Florence
Papal states
Genoa
Venice
Siena
km
0
100
N
GREECE
Athens

TIMELINE

A D
1425
1450
1475
1500
1525
1550
1575
1600

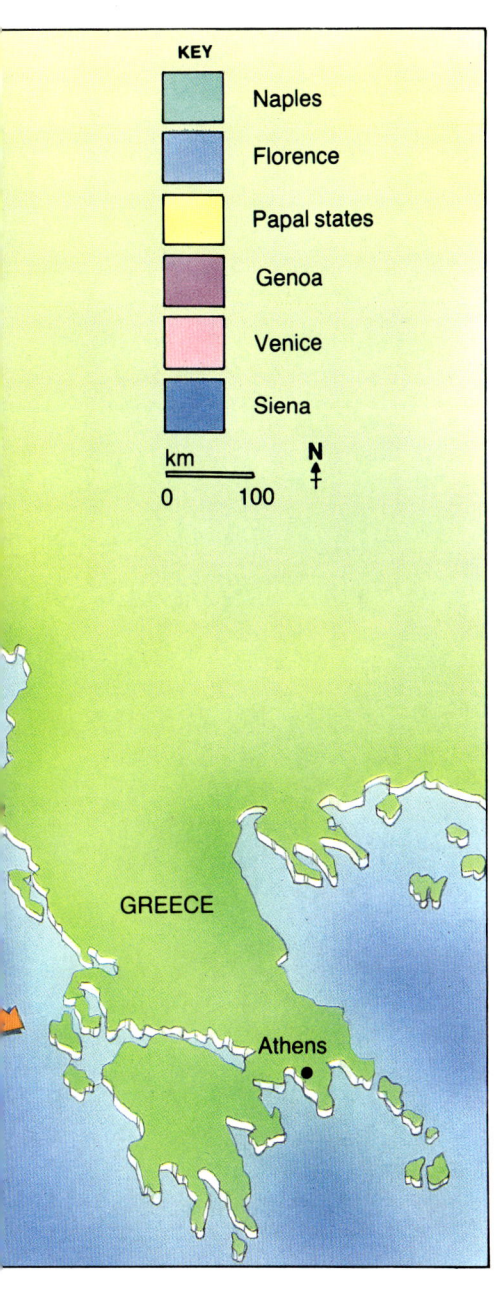

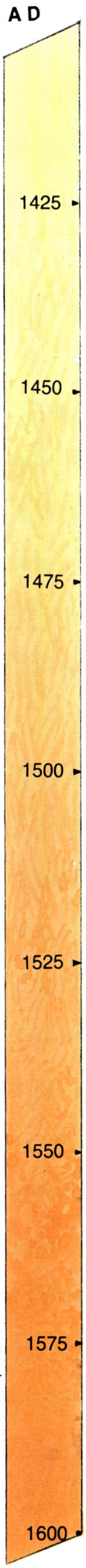

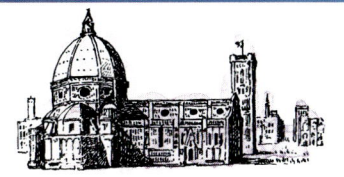

1423
Brunelleschi starts work on dome of Florence Cathedral

1434
Jan van Eyck paints 'The Marriage of Giovanni Arnolfini and Giovanna Cenami'

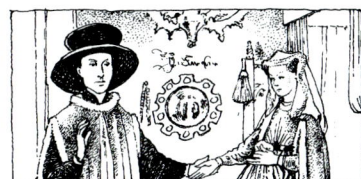

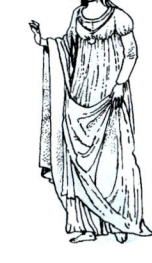

1477
Botticelli's 'Primavera'

1492
Columbus reaches America

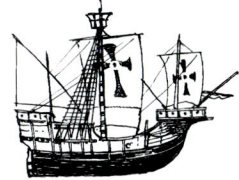

1503
'Mona Lisa' painted

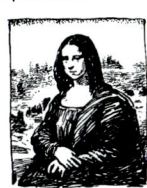

1519–1547
Chateau of Chambord built

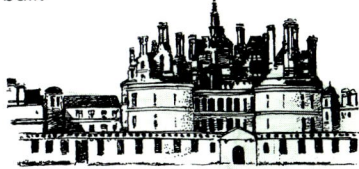

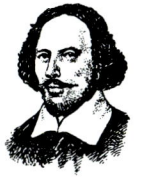

1590
Shakespeare's first plays performed in London

1426
Verrochio's statue of David

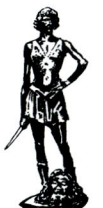

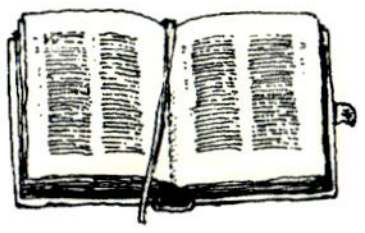

1450
First printed book (Gutenberg)

Lorenzo de' Medici (1449–1492)

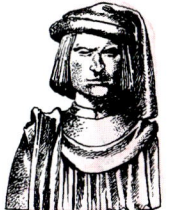

1492
Leonardo da Vinci's 'flying machine'

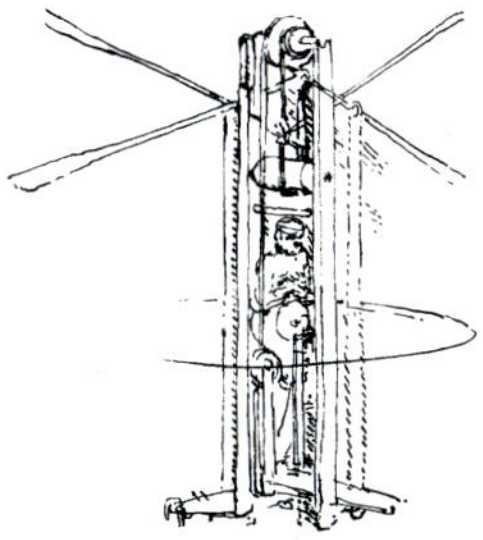

1508–1512
Michaelangelo paints Sistine Chapel

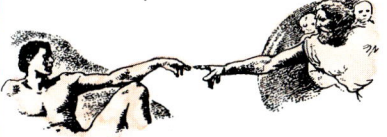

1539
Copernicus' ideas on solar system published

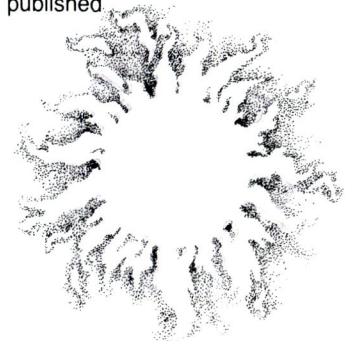

UNIT 1

A divided land

AIMS

In this unit we will look at life in Italy on the eve of the Renaissance, that is round about AD 1400. Who lived and worked there? Were they rich or poor? Who ruled there? Was the land peaceful, or was it divided by war? And what did citizens of other European states think about the Italian land and its people?

Today we think of Italy as just one country, stretching from the snowy Alps in the north to the sun-baked coastline of the south. But in 1400, and for hundreds of years before, the land of Italy was divided into dozens of separate states. Some of these states, like Venice or Genoa, were large and prosperous. They ruled vast areas of land, and maintained fleets of ships and armies of well-trained soldiers to defend their territories.

Other Italian states, like Urbino, were tiny. They contained just a walled city and the surrounding woods, pastures and fields. These smaller states often joined together in confederations, or made alliances with one of the larger states, to protect themselves.

There was often fighting between the Italian states, as each one struggled to gain control over its neighbours. Italy was also invaded by hostile troops from France, Spain, Greece and Turkey. They thought that because the land was divided, it would be easy to attack.

SOURCE 1
The rugged Italian landscape. This photo shows the countryside near the city of Florence, in central Italy.

SOURCE 2
A typical farm in northern Europe. This picture comes from an early 16th century manuscript painted in the Netherlands.

SOURCE 3
Florence, a typical Italian Renaissance city. This painting dates from 1561.

Natural hazards

As well as being divided by wars and quarrels, Italy was also divided by its geography. Much of the country was rocky and mountainous. It was difficult, and sometimes dangerous, to make long journeys overland. Other areas of Italy, like the rich, fertile northern river valleys, were swampy and sometimes flooded. They were also unhealthy. Swarms of mosquitoes bred there and spread disease to people and animals alike. These natural hazards encouraged the development of separate, independent communities, each fiercely proud of its own achievements. Each community was also bitterly resentful of any 'foreign' interference. Source 1 shows a typical landscape in Tuscany, the area around the city of Florence. You can see the isolated towns and villages clustered on some of the hilltops, as well as the rough, rocky roads connecting them.

Living in towns

In the rest of Europe, most people lived and worked in the countryside. Source 2 shows a typical northern European farm and the people who worked there. However, by 1400, most Italian people lived in towns. This was for three reasons: it was sociable, safer, and more profitable. Italian towns were usually surrounded by a strong outer wall; you can see an example in Source 3. Strangers could enter the town only through a well-built and well-defended gateway, which was locked at night.

Towns were also great centres of trade. Italian craft workers made high-quality goods (silk cloth, leather shoes, belts and bags, gold and silver jewellery and fragile glassware) that were prized throughout Europe. Merchants, bankers, scribes and shopkeepers all profited from this busy trade. Source 4 contains a description of an Italian city by 15th century visitors, and a popular Italian saying.

'The most triumphant city I have ever seen.'

'Honour does not dwell in the woods; worthy men are made in cities.'

SOURCE 4
The first comment is a description of Venice by the French chronicler, Philip de Comines, who visited the city during the late 15th century. The second is a 15th century proverb from Florence.

ACTIVITY

1. Imagine you were a traveller from Britain in early 15th century Tuscany. Choose three words to describe what your journey might have been like:
   a in summer, when the weather is hot and dry;
   b in winter, when it is cold and rainy.
2. Use Sources 1 and 3 to decide where you would have preferred to live in Renaissance Italy, town or country. Give reasons for your decision.

A DIVIDED LAND

SOURCE 5
The waterfront at Venice, as shown in an early 15th century manuscript.

SOURCE 6
A 15th century Italian merchant on the quayside.

Merchant cities

Some of the most powerful states in Renaissance Italy were centred on great trading cities. Two of these cities, Venice and Genoa, were ports. Their merchants and seamen travelled half-way round the world to bring back rare and precious goods from China, India, Central Asia, North Africa and the islands of the East Indies. They used the riches that they gained through trade to build many splendid buildings in their home cities. Source 5 shows a view of Venice from the sea; Source 6 portrays a well-dressed, wealthy Italian merchant on the quayside. His ship rides at anchor in the deep waters of the harbour, while close by, two sailors are filling sacks with grain.

A DIVIDED LAND

SOURCE 7
Medieval textile workers cutting material into a robe.

> The noble city called Venice, which is today the richest and pleasantest in the world, full of beauty and all good things. Merchandise flows through this city even as water flows from the fountains. . . . From all parts there come merchandise and merchants, who buy goods as they wish and take them back to their own countries. Within this town is found food in great plenty, bread and wine, land fowl and river fowl, fresh meat and salted meat, sea fish and river fish . . . you may find many men of gentle birth and money changers, and citizens of all crafts, and . . . mariners of all sorts, and ships to carry them to all lands.

SOURCE 8
A description of Venice in 1268, written by Martino da Canale, a proud citizen.

1. What do Sources 6 and 7 tell us about the clothes worn by wealthy people like merchants, and ordinary workers? List three ways in which their clothes were similar to one another, and three ways in which they were different.
2. Why do you think wealthy people in Renaissance Italy were prepared to spend large amounts of money on clothes?
3. Venice is a city built on the edge of water. How did its people obtain all the things mentioned in Source 8?

Silks, slaves and spices

The most valuable goods imported by Venetian and Genoese merchants were silks, spices, sugar, medicines, jewels, porcelain, dyestuffs and, shamefully, slaves. Venice was the centre of the silk and spice trade, while Genoa was the European headquarters of the trade in cotton, dyestuffs and other chemicals, and slaves. Historians think that about one in ten of the people living in Genoa during the 15th century had been bought there as a slave. Mostly, slaves came from north and east Africa and the Asian lands bordering the Black Sea. They were sold to Italian merchants by slave-traders from their own countries, or by salesmen based in the Muslim lands of the Middle East.

Local industries

Other Italian cities grew rich through manufacturing. The cloth industry, in particular, employed many people living in the towns. Workers cleaned raw silk and woollen fleeces, spun them into thread, wove them into elaborate designs, dyed them, trimmed and pressed them. The finished cloth was then tailored into elegant garments. Wealthy people ordered robes trimmed with gold and silver thread or costly fur. Some of the wool and silk used in the cloth industry came from Italy, but the finest quality raw materials were imported from distant lands. The best wool came from England and Spain, and silk came from China. You can see 14th century cloth workers in Source 7.

Craft guilds

Trade was carefully controlled, and taxed, by the city council (most of the wealthy merchants were city councillors). Day-to-day life in the workshops was organised through craft guilds. These protected the workers, by demanding fair wages and reasonable working conditions, and tried to ensure a high standard in all the goods produced. Each industry had its own separate guild. Only skilled workmen (and occasionally women) were allowed to join. Source 8 describes some of the many trades which flourished in 13th century Venice.

A DIVIDED LAND

Financial families

Italian cities also grew rich through the profits made by financial experts – bankers and money-lenders – who lived there. Source 9 shows an Italian banker at work in his office. Among the most famous of these bankers were the Medici dynasty, who lived in Florence. The Medici, and other 'financial families', lent money to merchants, provided safe places to store cash and valuables, and issued 'letters of credit' (rather like present-day cheques or postal orders). Merchants could carry these letters with them easily, instead of heavy, bulky coins. Paper money was unknown in Europe, although it was already in use in China.

Merchants paid for all these services, and their payments helped the Medici to get rich. The Church forbade usury (the lending of money for a fee). This practice is known today as 'charging interest'. But there were various ways of getting round this ban. In the 15th century, the Medici interest rates for deposits and loans were about the same as those charged by banks and building societies during the 1980s.

Banks and banking

The Medici set up branches of their banks in important trading cities throughout Europe. Source 10 shows the Medici bank in Milan, built in 1461 in the most up-to-date architectural style. Staff working in these banks made use of two new inventions: so-called 'arabic' numbers, and double entry book-keeping. Arabic numbers (the figures 0 to 9 which we use today) had been invented in India but were introduced into Europe by Muslim scholars working in Spain. They replaced the old Roman system and were easier and more accurate to use. Double entry book-keeping was a way of recording precisely what money a merchant had paid out, and what he had received. It helped businesses to keep better control of their accounts, to become more profitable.

SOURCE 9
Italian bankers and money-changers at work. The manuscript was painted in the 15th century.

SOURCE 10
The new building which housed the Medici bank in Milan. It was designed by the architect Michelozzo, and completed in 1461.

A DIVIDED LAND

Risky business

The Medici, and other rich people, used their wealth to make even more money by investing in new business ventures, called companies. Source 11 shows how the system worked. It could be a risky business – the companies did not always succeed – but it could also be very profitable. Successful merchants and bankers used the profits they made to spend lavishly on new houses, clothes, jewellery and entertainment. Source 12 shows a wealthy Italian family gathered for a meal. Prosperous citizens like these also became great patrons of Renaissance art. You can read more about this in unit 2.

> **attainment target 1**
>
> Look again at Source 11. Work with a partner or with the rest of your class and make sure you understand how the company system worked. Now answer these questions:
>
> 1. How do you think the company system encouraged trade?
>
> 2. Why do you think that merchants in Renaissance Italy were prepared to make the risky investment in trading companies?
>
> 3. Explain how and why the Medicis of Florence had become so rich.
>
> 4. Why do you think the Medici family chose to build the Milan branch of their bank (pictured in Source 10) in an elaborate, expensive and up-to-date style? Clue: imagine you were a merchant, looking for somewhere secure to leave your money, or that you were someone who wanted to borrow money from the bank. How would you feel as you walked towards this building?

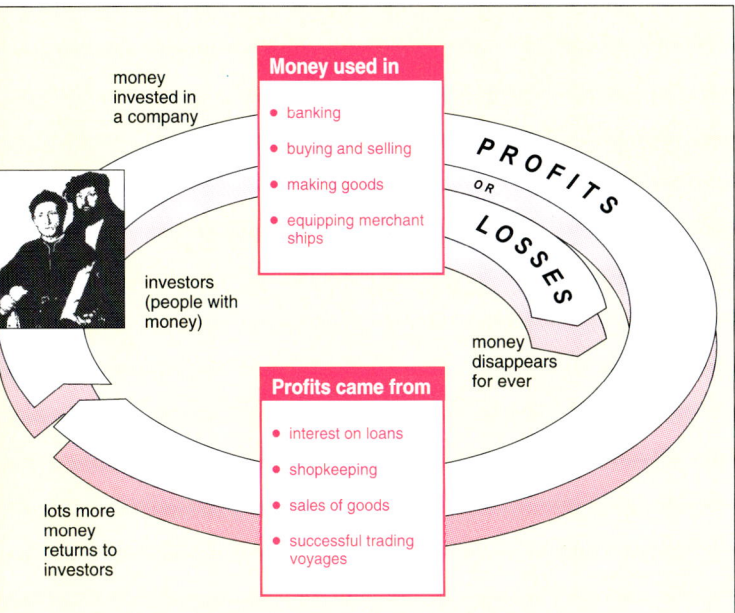

SOURCE 11
How an investment company worked.

SOURCE 12
A wealthy Italian family seated at table in their spacious, expensively decorated dining-room. This picture was painted early in the 16th century.

A DIVIDED LAND

The power of the Church

As we have seen, great cities, rich merchants and clever bankers were all very powerful in Italy on the eve of the Renaissance. There was another important Italian power: the Catholic Church, led by the POPE who lived in Rome. Source 13 shows Pope Sixtus IV with his COURTIERS. Apart from their clothing (the Pope wears a pointed crown and the courtiers wear CARDINAL's robes and hats), it is hard to tell the difference between the Pope and other Princes. Source 14 lists the names of the popes during the Renaissance period.

The Pope was bishop of Rome and leader of all Christians in western Europe at the time (Source 15). He was also the ruler of a large area in central Italy. Like other Italian rulers, Renaissance popes took a keen interest in learning and the arts. So much so that some religious thinkers accused them of being idle and neglecting their spiritual duties. This was not the only criticism directed at the 15th century Church. For many years, sincere Christians had been shocked when there were two or even three rival popes. Normally, a new pope was elected by the cardinals in secret discussions to choose the best man. But rulers from all over Europe tried to make the cardinals elect their own CANDIDATES. Control of the Pope would give them even more power. As a result, rival popes were sometimes elected by different groups of cardinals.

SOURCE 13
Sixtus IV (who was pope from 1471 to 1484) seated on his throne, with members of the papal court.

SOURCE 14
Popes at the time of the Renaissance. Those marked with (*) were famous for their support of Renaissance artists, architects and scholars.

Date elected	Name	Family	Home city
1417	Martin V	Colonna	Rome
1431	*Eugenius IV	Condulmaro	Venice
1439	Felix V		Duchy of Savoy
1447	*Nicholas V	Parentucelli	Sarzana
1455	Calixtus III	Borgia	Valencia, Spain
1458	*Pius II	Piccolomini	Siena
1464	*Paul II	Barbo	Venice
1471	*Sixtus IV	delle Rovere	Savona
1484	Innocent VIII	Cibo	Genoa
1492	*Alexander VI	Borgia	Valencia/Bologna
1503	Pius III		
1503	*Julius II	delle Rovere	Savona
1513	*Leo X	de' Medici	Florence
1522	*Adrian VI	Dedel	Utrecht, Netherlands
1533	*Clement VII	de' Medici	Florence
1534	*Paul III	Farnese	Florence/Rome

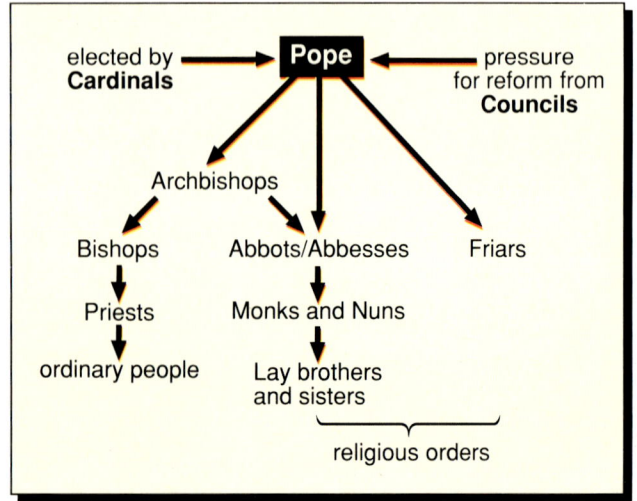

SOURCE 15
The power structure of the Catholic Church in the 15th century.

The great councils

Although this period of rival popes came to an end in 1417, there were still major arguments within the Church. Leading clergymen called for more control over the powers of the pope, and for a reform of Church government. They met at a series of great councils to discuss how Church organisation might be improved (Source 16).

People were also dismayed at how the city of Rome had been allowed to decay (see Source 17).

SOURCE 16
A session of the Council of Constance in Constance Cathedral, in 1415.

'Oh God, how much is Rome to be pitied.'

SOURCE 17
Comment on the state of Rome by the British traveller, Adam of Usk, who visited the city in the late 14th century.

Renaissance popes

The popes who led the Church during the Renaissance were mostly very capable. Many of them were clever politicians and some were great scholars, but they did not lead 'holy' lives. They were almost all chosen from Italian noble families. The Church offered their younger sons a good 'career', and the chance of winning fame, money and political power. Source 18 shows a young Italian nobleman who has just been made a cardinal (a position of great power), surrounded by his family.

SOURCE 18
A painting by Andrea Mantegna, completed in 1474. It portrays the leader of a rich, noble family in Mantua welcoming home his son, who has just been made a cardinal.

ACTIVITY

1. In what ways do the Church leaders in Sources 13 and 18 look like princes, not priests?

2. Why do you think leading Italian families would want one of their members to be elected Pope?

3. Do you think it is right or wrong for the Church to spend money on paintings and architecture?

A DIVIDED LAND

SOURCE 19
A typical 14th century Italian painting: 'The Annunciation' by Simone Martini and Lippo Memmi, completed in 1333.

Arts and learning

Princes, popes, rich citizens and travelling merchants living in Italy on the eve of the Renaissance had money to spend. They bought books and pictures, and gave money to universities and to fund exploration and science. This generous spending had results: painting, literature and scholarship flourished. There were many problems facing people in late 14th century Italy, such as PLAGUE, ECONOMIC DEPRESSION and war. Even so, wealthy Italians continued to support learning and the arts. By doing this, they helped to lay the foundations for all the later achievements of the Renaissance.

'You were not made to live the lives of brutes But rather to seek virtue and to learn.'

SOURCE 20
Lines written by the Italian poet, Alighieri Dante (1265–1321).

A DIVIDED LAND

The old and the new

Source 19 shows a typical late-medieval painting. It is by Martini and Memmi, two artists who lived and worked in Siena, a walled city not far from Florence. Like most medieval painters, they chose a religious subject. They used precious materials, such as goldleaf and paint made from a powdered jewel-stone called lapis lazuli, to create a beautiful, holy object. The picture is painted in medieval artistic 'shorthand'; only the main characters (the Virgin Mary and the angel Gabriel) are shown. There is no background scenery, and no lifelike colour, shape or detail. The Virgin Mary and the angel are painted as religious SYMBOLS, not as real people. The painting was designed to create a holy mood, not to record everyday people, places and things. Medieval churchgoers who saw the picture would also have recognised that the lilies in the vase were a sign, or symbol, of Mary's purity.

Source 21 shows another typically medieval picture, a page from a 14th century Italian 'herbal' (book about plants and their medicinal uses). Like the painting in Source 19, it is not realistic: the plants and figures are not drawn to scale; the onion is as big as the woman; and the boys in the cherry-tree look like miniature adults.

New techniques

Italian artists, scholars and writers were famous throughout Europe. By the late 14th century, many of them were beginning to experiment with new themes for poems and paintings, or with new artistic techniques. Source 20 is a quotation from one of the best known Italian medieval poets. It is an example of the new ideas which helped the Renaissance to develop. The medieval Church taught that people should live holy lives in the hope of winning a place in Heaven. But here, instead, Dante suggests that people should seek virtue for its own sake, and devote themselves to learning.

1 Look in your school or local library and find books with pictures of people and vegetables. They could be cookery books or books about gardening. Compare their layout and illustrations with those of Source 21. Complete this sentence: 'Two important differences between medieval and modern illustrations are _____ and _____.'

2 In Source 20, the writer contrasts human beings with brutes, or animals. With the rest of your class, discuss whether or not you agree with him. Is humanity better than other living creatures, or just more powerful and ruthless?

SOURCE 21
Page from a book about medicinal plants, written and illustrated in northern Italy, late 14th century. This drawing shows a woman and two boys picking cherries, and an onion plant in flower.

UNIT 2

Princes and patrons

AIMS

In this unit we shall look at some of the powerful men and women who ruled the rich Italian city-states. What were their aims? How did they govern? Why did they spend vast sums of money on encouraging new art and architecture? Finally, did everyone approve of what they were doing?

As we saw in unit 1, Italy in the 15th century was a divided land. The city-states were rivals. Each one struggled to outdo its neighbours in making profits from trade and in conquering new territory. They were often at war. These harsh facts shaped the policies of the men (and the few women) who governed the Italian city-states. First and foremost, they aimed to protect trade and to keep out invaders.

The rulers of Italy had other aims, as well. They hoped to win fame and glory for themselves and to increase the PRESTIGE of their cities. This was not only enjoyable, it also brought certain advantages. People respected famous leaders, and would think twice before attacking a city-state which they believed to be well-led, strong and prosperous. At home, too, there were benefits. Citizens would support a leader who helped to secure prosperity and peace. They could take pride in their town's strength and reputation, and perhaps make a profit from it. Source 1 shows a festival procession, displaying the city's wealth and power, passing through the streets of Venice. Public displays like this, which attracted visitors (with money to spend), were often followed by sports, feasting and drinking.

SOURCE 1
A glittering procession led by the Doge (leader of the city-state) of Venice. This picture was painted by Giovanni Bellini in 1496.

Avoiding fighting

Renaissance leaders aimed to prevent fighting if at all possible. Wars were brutal (see Source 2), bloodthirsty and very expensive. Men were killed, women were widowed and children were left fatherless. Wars also interfered with trade and cost money. Strong walls had to be built around each city (see Source 3). Paying high prices for weapons, armour and specially trained mercenaries (hired soldiers) could bring a city-state to near BANKRUPTCY. Even so, people living in 15th and 16th century Italy believed that it was important to spend money on weapons, as Source 4 reveals.

Peaceful war

Surprisingly, art could be used to help prevent fighting. Each city-state aimed to rival its neighbours by displaying its latest artistic and architectural treasures. This not only impressed important visitors, but was also politically useful.

SOURCE 2
'The Battle of San Romano', painted by Paolo Uccello around 1456.

SOURCE 3
The strong walls of Florence, shown in a manuscript of 1440.

> The main foundations of every state . . . are good laws and good arms; . . . you cannot have good laws without good arms, and where there are good arms, good laws inevitably follow. . . .

SOURCE 4
From Niccolò Machiavelli's famous book *The Prince*, written in 1513–1514.

Look again at Source 4. Work with a partner to make sure you understand the meaning of this text, then answer the following questions. (NB 'arms' means 'weapons'.)

1. Which does the writer of Source 4 (Machiavelli) think is more important to a city-state – good weapons or good laws?
2. Why does he think this?
3. Do you agree with Machiavelli? Give reasons.

PRINCES AND PATRONS

A good prince?

If you were the ruler of an Italian city-state in the 14th century, how would you try to make people admire and respect you? Probably, as we saw on pages 16–17, you would make sure your city was well-defended. You would be strong-minded, and act DECISIVELY. You would do what you could to protect and encourage trade. Perhaps you would help poor and sick people, as the Church said you should. If you were wise, you would consult with the wealthier and more powerful citizens. In that way, you would stop them trying to seize power for themselves. You might also encourage ordinary people to bring their problems to you.

All this commonsense advice was given to rulers in Renaissance Italy by writers living at that time. But some Renaissance advice was surprising. Look at Source 5. It was written by the governor of an important Italian city. Would you have chosen to build a magnificent house just because it was politically necessary?

'It is the work of a magnificent man to construct a fine dwelling, for people who see marvellous buildings are deeply impressed with strong admiration....'

SOURCE 5
Comment by Azzo Visconti, who ruled as Lord of Milan during the mid-14th century.

SOURCE 6
Federico da Montefeltro and his wife Battista Sforza, rulers of the city-state of Urbino – painted by Piero della Francesca in 1472.

SOURCE 7
Courtyard of the DUCAL palace, Urbino, designed by the architect Laurana (1420–1479).

PRINCES AND PATRONS

Pleasure and patronage

Most Renaissance rulers would have agreed with Azzo Visconti (Source 5) that a fine house was important for political reasons. However, many Renaissance rulers were also willing to spend money on art and architecture simply because it interested or pleased them.

Some wealthy rulers, like Federico da Montefeltro and his wife Battista Sforza (pictured in Source 6), were extremely generous patrons of the arts. They collected pictures, manuscripts, books, furniture, jewellery and other lovely objects. They COMMISSIONED an elegant new palace, where they could display their treasures (see Source 7). Like another great patron, Isabella d'Este (you can see her in Source 8), the Montefeltros made friends with famous artists, writers and musicians. They invited them to stay at their courts. Also like Isabella, they became familiar with the different styles and subjects of Renaissance art. As Source 9 suggests, Isabella could write about pictures and discuss them with knowledge and understanding.

SOURCE 8
Isabella d'Este (1474-1539), a famous Italian noblewoman. She was a knowledgeable and generous patron to many writers, musicians and artists. This portrait is by Leonardo da Vinci.

SOURCE 9
Letter from Isabella d'Este to the artist Leonardo da Vinci, 1504.

> Master Leonardo – hearing that you are staying in Florence, we . . . hope that something we have long desired might come true: to have something (painted or drawn) by your hand. . . . Do a youthful Christ of about 12 years old . . . carried out with that sweetness and soft . . . charm which only you can do so excellently. If you can fulfil this strong craving of ours to our satisfaction, you will know that beyond the payment, which you yourself can fix, we shall remain so obliged to you that we shall think of nothing else but to do you good service. . . .
> Expecting a favourable reply. . . .

ACTIVITY

Look at the pictures of Federico da Montefeltro and Battista Sforza in Source 6. Even if you did not know they were powerful rulers, the portraits contain 'clues' which tell you that they were important people.

1. Write down at least two different clues you can spot in each picture.

2. Write a sentence to explain why you think these two people wanted their portraits painted.

3. These paintings have survived for over 400 years. If you were commissioning a picture of yourself designed to last that long, how would you want to be shown? Consider your pose, clothing, expression, surroundings and the materials the portrait would be made from.

PRINCES AND PATRONS

Fine cities

Wealthy rulers were not the only people in 15th century Italy to take an interest in buildings, painting and sculpture. Citizens of the thriving Italian city-states (such as Florence, shown in Source 10) also wanted to make their surroundings as beautiful and as comfortable as possible. Source 11 tells us that the ordinary citizens of Florence were also keen to win for themselves a share of 'glory and honour' by paying for works of art.

Why spend money?

In Source 12, Giovanni Rucellai explains why this was so. It was partly for religious reasons: priests taught that gifts given to the Church helped people gain forgiveness for their sins, and secure a place in Heaven. It was partly for the honour of the city: each elegant new building benefited the community as a whole, and most Florentines were fiercely proud and patriotic. Some citizens believed that people were encouraged by their fine surroundings to live better, nobler lives. Having new, clean and beautiful buildings around you was pleasant, but it could also be inspiring. Lastly, a work of art could serve as a MEMORIAL, not only to its creator, but also to the person who paid for it.

SOURCE 10
Typical street scene in Florence, painted about 1530 by Francesco Ubertini.

'In that city (Florence) men are driven on by three things: disapproval . . . never being content with second best but seeking what is good and beautiful; hard work . . . and being shrewd and quick in their dealings and knowing how to earn money; . . . and by a quest for glory and honour. . . .'

SOURCE 11
Analysis of the character of Florentine citizens by Giorgio Vasari (1511–1574), an Italian painter, architect and historian.

> I have also spent a great deal of money on my house and on the . . . Church of Santa Maria Novella and on the chapel of San Pancrazio (and on other gifts to churches and on fine buildings and gardens). All the above-mentioned things have given me the greatest satisfaction and pleasure, because in part they serve the honour of God as well as the honour of the city and the COMMEMORATION of myself . . . I have done nothing for the last 50 years but earn and spend . . . I have had the greatest pleasure and satisfaction from both, and I really think it is even more pleasurable to spend than to earn. . . .'

SOURCE 12
Written by Giovanni Rucellai, a successful Florentine merchant, in 1473.

PRINCES AND PATRONS

Gifts and competitions

The merchant Giovanni Rucellai, who gave so much money to help beautify his home city of Florence, freely chose to do so. No one forced him to be generous, although most people expected that merchants who had made money working in the city would want to give something back.

Sometimes the leading citizens decided to encourage the construction of new buildings to bring further prestige to the community. For example, in Florence in the early 15th century they arranged a competition to design new bronze doors for the Baptistery (chapel where newborn babies were christened). Source 13 shows one panel from the winning entry. As you can see, the standard of design and craftsmanship was very high. At around the same time, another ambitious new building project was in progress: the vast new dome for a major city landmark, Florence Cathedral (shown in Source 14).

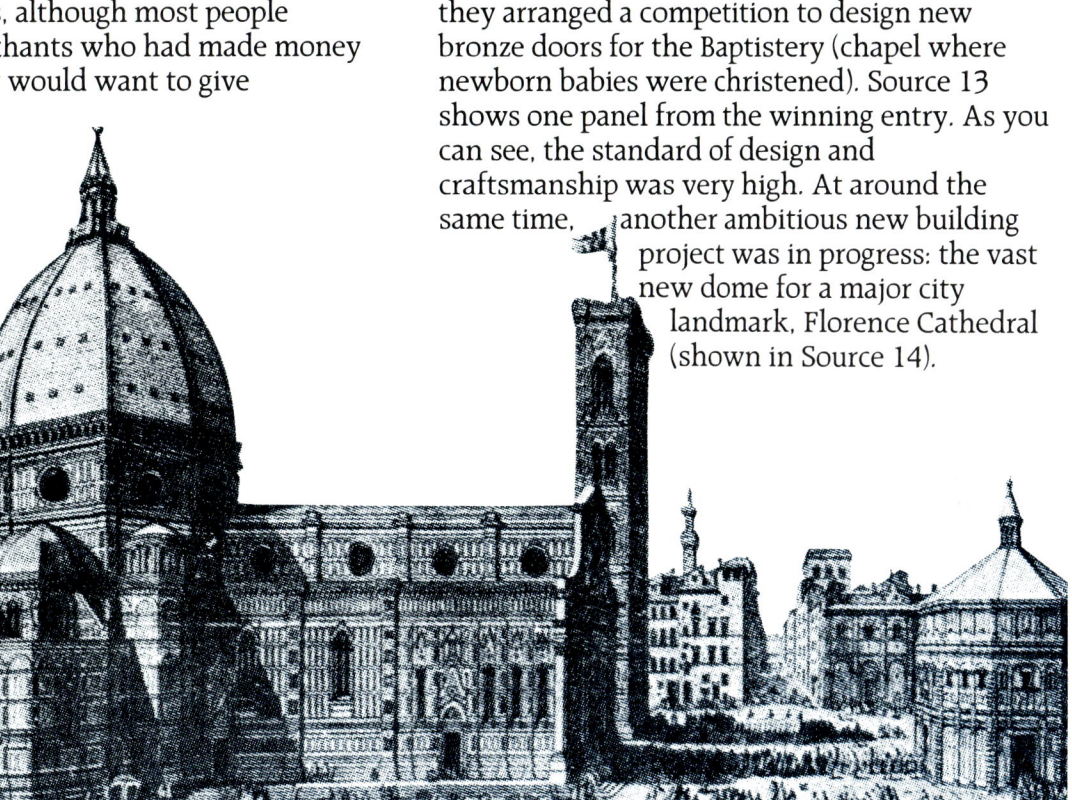

SOURCE 14
The magnificent dome of Florence Cathedral, designed by Filippo Brunelleschi and completed in the mid-15th century. It was a great feat of engineering.

SOURCE 13
Winning design for the doors of the Baptistery in Florence, made by Lorenzo Ghiberti in 1401–1402.

1 Look again at Source 12. Give one example of fact from Rucellai's letter, and one example of opinion.

2 What were Rucellai's motives for spending money?

3 This is just one person's account. How useful is it to us in finding out about the Renaissance?

4 From what you have read in this unit so far, how typical do you think Rucellai was?

5 Do you think it is more fun to spend than to earn?

PRINCES AND PATRONS

'The cradle of the Renaissance'?

We have already seen how several important houses and churches in Florence were redecorated or rebuilt in the early 15th century. Hundreds of years later, some writers called Florence 'the cradle of the Renaissance' (see also page 28). What does this mean? Is it true? And if so, how did it happen?

By describing Florence as 'the cradle of the Renaissance', those later writers meant two things: firstly, that the Renaissance had started (or had been 'born') in the city; secondly, that it had provided a welcoming, secure environment (like a baby's cradle) in which the newborn Renaissance could flourish.

True or false?

These claims were only partly true. It is not accurate to say that the Renaissance started only in Florence. Today many historians think that Renaissance ideas began to develop in many centres throughout Italy, and elsewhere in Europe, at around the same time. (This is discussed more fully in unit 4, pages 50 to 59.) However, most historians do agree that conditions in 15th century Florence provided a 'cradle' in which art, architecture and learning could flourish.

> Florence is 'very free... everyone talks a lot, some in favour, some uncertain, and others pursuing their own different interests....'

SOURCE 15
Comment on political life in Florence by Bartolommeo Scala, a leading city official, in 1469.

There were several reasons for this. The people of Florence prided themselves on their freedom (see Source 15). They were therefore likely to welcome new ideas. The leading family in Florence, the Medici (see Source 17), were immensely wealthy, energetic and powerful. They were also great patrons of the arts. Led by Cosimo de' Medici (Source 16), who took control of the city in the mid-15th century, they worked hard to enrich themselves. At the same time, this private wealth brought public glory. The Medici demanded (and could pay for) the very best, so they encouraged the most skilful, creative and original artists and architects to come and work for them in Florence. Sources 18 and 19 show examples of what some of these Renaissance artists achieved.

SOURCE 16
Cosimo de' Medici as an old man. This medal was made around 1464, the year of his death.

SOURCE 17
The Medici dynasty: the most powerful family in Florence from 1421. Those who became rulers of Florence are shown in **bold**.

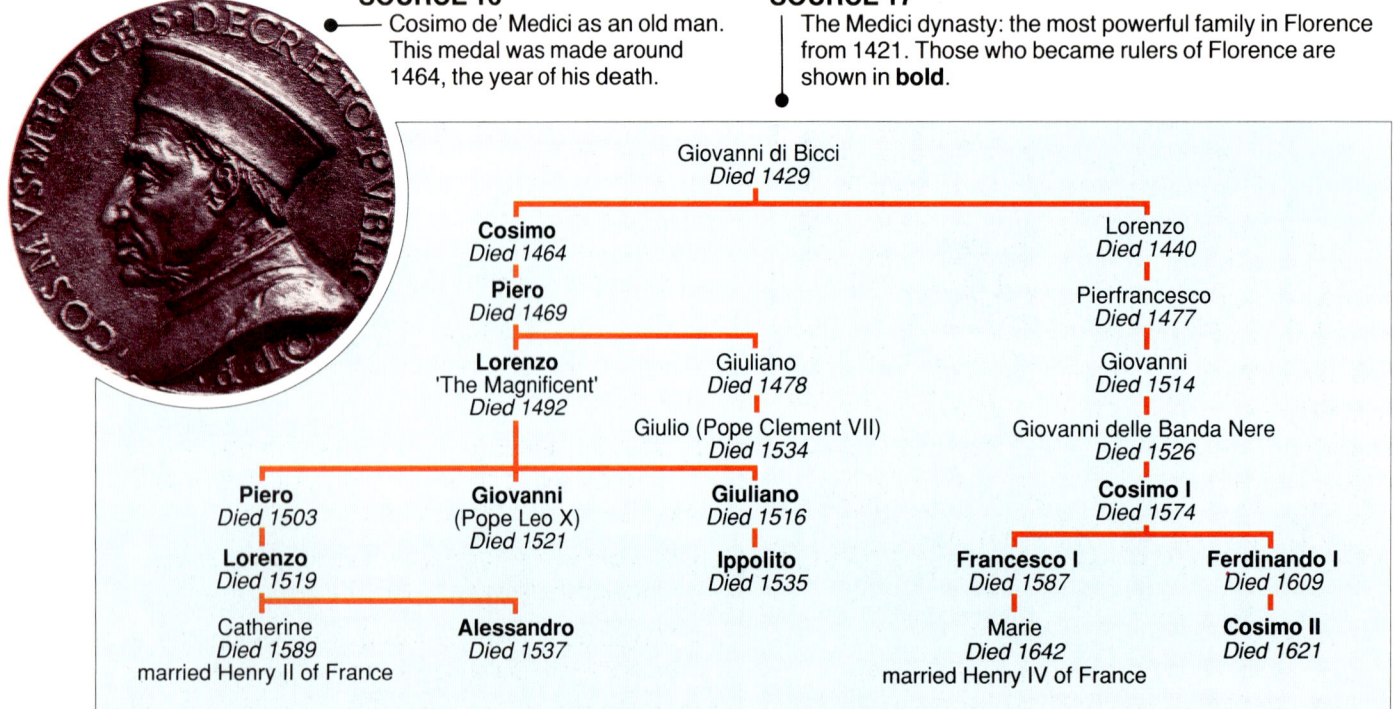

SOURCE 18
Painting by Benozzo Gozzoli in the chapel of the Medici palazzo in Florence (see Source 19), completed in 1459.

SOURCE 19
Large house, or 'palazzo', in Florence designed for Cosimo de' Medici by the architect Michelozzo in 1444.

attainment target 1

freedom of ideas in Florence
wealth of Florence
personality of Cosimo de' Medici
rivalry of cities
lots of talented artists

1. Choose three of these factors and explain how they helped Florence become 'the cradle of the Renaissance'.

2. What differences are there between these five factors, for instance is one political, one financial, one personal, one artistic etc.?

3. Why did all five of these factors come together in Florence in the early 15th century?

4. Do you agree with the view that money was the crucial factor that made the Renaissance possible?

PRINCES AND PATRONS

After Cosimo

Cosimo de' Medici died in 1464. His successor, Piero de' Medici, was weak and sickly. He died in 1469, leaving his 21 year-old son, Lorenzo (pictured in Source 20), to take charge of Florence. Lorenzo's journal (quoted in Source 21) describes his feelings on coming to power. Many other people living at that time must have shared his doubts and fears.

Lorenzo ruled for over 20 years. Few people would have dared to predict that his 'reign' would turn out well. Florence was a republic, without kings or princes; so, in theory, the Medici family were only ordinary citizens, like everyone else. But Lorenzo proved very skilful at keeping hold of power. He worked with Florentine officials to ensure the smooth running of the city government.

Although Lorenzo has been widely praised, recently and in the past (see Source 22), he was also frequently criticised. Because he could be ruthless, he had enemies. Some citizens and many rival rulers resented the Medici power. There was a great scandal when Pope Sixtus IV had Lorenzo's brother murdered in church, after they had quarrelled.

SOURCE 20
Portrait of Lorenzo de' Medici (known as Lorenzo 'The Magnificent') made of terracotta (fired clay) around 1485.

SOURCE 21
From Lorenzo de' Medici's diary, written in 1469.

> The second day after (my father's) death, although I was very young, being 21 years of age, the principal men of the City and the State came to our house to offer their sympathy and to persuade me to take charge . . . as my father and my grandfather had done. I agreed, but unwillingly, because the responsibility and danger were great and I was so young. I did so in order to protect our friends and property, since at Florence life is insecure for the wealthy unless they control the government.

'Imagine (some)one who combined the functions (duties) of a Prime Minister, a banker and business MAGNATE, a Lord Mayor, a director of national galleries and museums, a president of the national ACADEMY, and a CHANCELLOR of two universities . . . .'

'This man has lived long enough for his own immortal fame, but not long enough for Italy.'

'Every day we shall learn more what we have lost.'

SOURCE 22
Tributes to Lorenzo de' Medici (from the top):
- by a 20th century historian, Harold Acton;
- by King Ferrante of Naples, Lorenzo's former enemy;
- by a 15th century Florentine writer, Bartolommeo Dei.

Lorenzo 'The Magnificent'

Today most people remember Lorenzo not for his political activities, but as a generous and imaginative patron of the arts. Life at his court was CULTURED and EXTRAVAGANT. He also provided lavish public entertainments.

During Lorenzo's years in power, Florence became a great centre of learning and artistic experiment. New, beautiful and, sometimes, astonishing works of art (Sources 23 and 24 are just two examples) graced private houses and public open spaces. (You can find out why they were so astonishing by reading unit 3.) Artists, scholars, musicians, architects and philosophers met daily around Lorenzo's dinner table to discuss their ideas with leading Florentine citizens and with Lorenzo himself.

PRINCES AND PATRONS

SOURCE 23
A statue in bronze portraying the Biblical hero David who killed the giant, Goliath. It was made around 1476 by Andrea del Verrochio.

ACTIVITY

Get into groups of 4 to 6. One of you is Lorenzo de' Medici; the rest are talented artists, architects and writers (see Source 20). One could be a visitor from another Italian state. Lorenzo has just come to power, and is deciding how he will rule. The group draw up the following, with 'Lorenzo' chairing the discussion:

- a list of things to do (you may find the text on page 18 useful here)
- some ideas on what kind of ruler to be
- some artistic and architectural schemes to astonish and impress the people of Florence and all Lorenzo's rivals throughout Italy.

The job of the visitor is to ask the question 'Why?' so that the Florentines present have to give their reasons.

[Note: This situation would not have happened in real life as Lorenzo de' Medici would not have discussed policy and politics with artists. Also a foreign visitor is unlikely to have been allowed to take part in any such discussion.]

SOURCE 24
'Primavera' ('Spring'), a painting by Sandro Botticelli, one of the artists employed at Lorenzo's court. It was completed in 1478.

PRINCES AND PATRONS

The road to Hell

Not everyone in Italy approved of the artistic achievements encouraged by Lorenzo de' Medici and other patrons. To the preacher FRIAR Savonarola (pictured in Source 25), works of art were 'vanities' – traps set by the Devil to drag people down to Hell. St Bernardino (quoted in Source 26) argued that 'worldly' things, even church buildings, were not really important in the eyes of God.

The only art that Savonarola approved of was religious art. Even that, he said, must be strictly controlled. Source 27 quotes one of Savonarola's sermons criticising Florentine religious paintings. Source 28 shows an example of the kind of art he objected so strongly to.

SOURCE 25
The Florentine preacher Friar Girolamo Savonarola (1452–1498).

'God loves one soul more than all the churches in the world.'

SOURCE 26
Comment by St Bernardino of Siena, another popular preacher in Italy in the 15th century.

SOURCE 28
A nativity painting by Domenico Ghirlandaio, painted in 1485.

> ... you have pictures in churches painted in the likeness of living women, which is wicked, and in great dishonour of what is God's. You painters do an evil thing.... Do you believe the Virgin Mary went dressed this way, as you paint her? I tell you, she went dressed simply, as a poor woman, and so covered that her face could hardly be seen.... You would do well to cover up these figures that you have painted so scandalously. You make the Virgin Mary seem dressed like a WHORE....

SOURCE 27
Part of a sermon preached by Savonarola to the people of Florence.

PRINCES AND PATRONS

SOURCE 29
The execution of Savonarola in the main square (the Piazza della Signoria) in Florence, 1498.

Fires and flames

Savonarola was active in Florence between 1482 and 1498. Large crowds came to hear him preach. He was fearless in DENOUNCING everyone in power, including the Pope and Lorenzo de' Medici. He urged people to throw away their books, pictures, fine clothes and furnishings, and return to a simple, holy life. He organised huge 'bonfires of vanities'. Citizens hurled their treasured possessions into the flames, as a sign of their devotion to God.

For a time, Savonarola set up a rival government in Florence, to challenge the city authorities. At first, he was protected by Lorenzo de' Medici, who listened with interest to what he had to say. Then Savonarola quarrelled publicly with the leaders of the Church. He was tried, sentenced to death and executed as a HERETIC in Florence's main square (Source 29).

Savonarola's 'reign of terror' in Florence was brief, but it was also important. It reminds us that Renaissance art was not only beautiful, nor was it simply an expensive STATUS SYMBOL. Rather, it had the power to arouse deep emotions, both for and against. People like Savonarola were willing to die in the effort to oppose it. In unit 3 you will find out what Renaissance artists were trying to achieve, and why their work was so powerful and, sometimes, so shocking.

> **attainment target 2**
>
> Look back at Source 22 on page 24 and compare these comments with Sources 26 and 27. Now answer these questions.
>
> 1 Give two examples of fact and two examples of opinion from these Sources.
>
> 2 Is Source 26 an example of fact or opinion?
>
> 3 What facts about Medici patronage and Renaissance art does the speaker in Source 27 seem to ignore?
>
> 4 Explain how Source 28 supports the view of Renaissance art given in Source 27.
>
> 5 If we only had Sources 26 and 27 to go on how might our interpretation of Renaissance art be different?
>
> 6 Why do you think modern historians (e.g. top comment, Source 22) feel differently about the achievements of Lorenzo de' Medici than St Bernardino and Savonarola did?

> 1 Why do you think Savonarola dared to speak out and criticise powerful people like Lorenzo de' Medici and the Pope?
>
> 2 Why do you think Savonarola won popular support among the ordinary people of Florence?

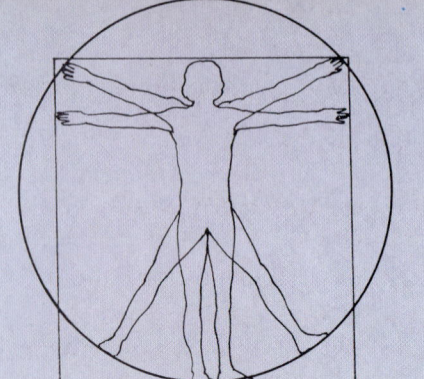

UNIT 3

A rebirth of art

AIMS

So far in this book we have seen that 15th century Italy provided a 'cradle' in which the arts could flourish. In this unit we shall look at Renaissance art itself. What was it like? How did it differ from art in earlier centuries? Who were the artists, architects, writers, scholars, scientists and philosophers who lived in Renaissance Italy? How did they work and what were they aiming to achieve?

All art, wherever it comes from, is produced in a particular style. It doesn't just 'happen'; it is the result of choices made by an artist about how he or she is going to spread paint over canvas, draw with a pencil on paper, or carve a block of wood or stone. Today we find that some styles change very quickly in painting, clothes and music. Think of some styles in clothes or music that you admired a year ago but no longer like today. How quickly do your tastes change?

This was not always so. In the past, styles changed slowly and gradually. There were few 'revolutions' in art.

Renaissance style

But to writers in the 16th century, a revolution in artistic style did seem to have taken place. They contrasted the art created in Italy (and a few other countries in Europe) between 1400 and 1500 with what had been produced in earlier centuries. The change was so striking that in 1550 one writer, Giorgio Vasari, chose the word '*rinascati*' (rebirth) to describe it. The same word ('Renaissance' in French and English) has been used ever since.

SOURCE 1
The Portinari ALTARPIECE (a picture designed to stand behind the altar in a church), painted by Hugo van der Goes around 1475. It was purchased by the wealthy Portinari family, and was the first important painting in the Netherlands style to be displayed in Florence.

Reproducing reality

What was so revolutionary about Renaissance art? In this unit you will see that it differed from the art of previous centuries in style, TECHNIQUE, subject matter and in what it was trying to achieve. One of the most important differences between Renaissance and medieval art was in its approach to showing 'reality' (that is, things as they are, or how they look).

Renaissance artists, in northern Europe and in Italy, were trying to make their pictures appear 'real'. Source 1 shows an example of art from the NETHERLANDS. The objects painted, especially the flowers in the foreground, are so lifelike that we feel we could almost touch them. Because we are so used to seeing photographs and television, this 'REALISM' may not seem very special to us today. But in the 15th century, when Source 1 was painted, it caused a sensation. Turn back to page 15 and look again at Source 21. Compare this painting with Source 1 opposite. Try to imagine the impact that this new, realistic painting must have had.

Other artists used different techniques to imitate reality. Sources 2 and 3 show how Masaccio, an Italian artist, copied real buildings to create an illusion of depth on the flat surface of a chapel wall in Florence. Framed by a realistic archway, a holy scene is taking place alongside people who have come to pray.

'He recognised that painting is nothing but the IMITATION of things as they are.'

SOURCE 3
Comment on Masaccio's new style of painting by the art historian Giorgio Vasari, who lived in Italy in the 16th century.

SOURCE 2
A FRESCO showing the Holy Trinity from the church of Santa Maria Novella, Florence. It was painted by Masaccio around 1427. The DONORS are shown at the front, kneeling.

ACTIVITY

Imagine that you are a Florentine citizen, seeing Masaccio's painting on the wall of your local church (Source 2) for the first time. What would your reaction be? Work with a partner, or in a small group, to write a short scene in which a group of citizens meet outside the church after a service. They talk about family news and gossip, but soon begin to discuss the new painting. Some like it; others disapprove. All have strongly-held opinions, and are prepared to argue about their reasons for holding them. Act out this scene in front of other members of the class.

A REBIRTH OF ART

Copying, distance and space

The artists who painted the pictures shown on pages 28 and 29 both used the same technique to imitate reality. They made detailed, accurate copies of things as they saw them. Their new way of copying was soon followed by another artistic discovery: the ability to portray space and distance in paintings by the use of PERSPECTIVE.

Medieval 'cartoons'

Look at Source 4. It is a typical medieval picture, showing seated monks listening to a preacher. The medieval artist who painted Source 4 was undoubtedly skilful. He has created an attractive picture, using bright colours and bold, swirling lines. But the style is not realistic; it is DISTORTED, like a modern cartoon. As the preacher is the most important person in the picture, the artist has made him almost twice as big as the audience. The seated monks appear to be crowded one on top of another. The artist has not tried to show space or distance.

SOURCE 4
A 12th century manuscript painting, in typical medieval style.

SOURCE 5
Fresco by an unknown painter from Florence, known as the Master of the Chiostro degli Aranci, painted between 1435 and 1440. It illustrates a scene from the life of St Benedict, who is shown here giving food to a raven.

A REBIRTH OF ART

SOURCE 6
In this painting (which shows Jesus Christ being whipped), the artist, Piero della Francesco, has used the Renaissance technique of perspective drawing to create a sense of distance and space. Perspective lines drawn on top of the painting (inset) show how the viewer's eye is led 'into' the picture.

Renaissance 'reality'

Now compare Source 4 with Source 5, which was painted during the early Renaissance. It shows a similar scene of seated monks, but there is a big difference. The Renaissance artist has learned how to show real space and distance. The whole scene seems much more true to life.

Planned perspective

Source 6 illustrates how this was done. It shows a skilful Renaissance painting, and the way in which it was planned. Renaissance artists discovered that by constructing their pictures around a VANISHING POINT (where all the lines meet), they could produce an illusion of lifelike space and distance. As the lines move outward from the vanishing point, the gap between them increases. Renaissance artists used these gaps as a guide for the size of people and objects shown in their pictures. As in real life, the closer something is to the spectator, the larger it appears. Compare the size of the people in the foreground of Source 6 with those shown in the distance, and you will see how this technique of perspective works.

> 1. Look again at Sources 4 and 5. Why do you think the medieval artist who designed Source 4 drew and painted it in the way he did?
> 2. To modern eyes, realism does not always make for an attractive picture, although it was highly praised in Renaissance times. In small groups, discuss which of Sources 4 and 5 you prefer. Give reasons for your choice.

A REBIRTH OF ART

The natural world

For medieval people, the natural world was something to be feared, rather than admired. They knew only too well that their crops might be destroyed by DROUGHT, flood or disease, or their farm animals carried off by wolves or bears. Of course, many people, then as now, enjoyed spring flowers and summer sunshine. Some medieval preachers, like St Francis of Assisi, taught that we should respect all plants and animals because, like us, they were part of God's creation.

Most medieval scholars, however, did not study nature. In many medieval texts illustrations of plants and animals were copied from earlier manuscripts rather than from real-life specimens. The Church discouraged the investigation of God's mysteries. It even forbade cutting up dead people by doctors who wanted to find out how the body worked.

SOURCE 7
Drawing of a plant by Leonardo da Vinci, made between 1505 and 1508.

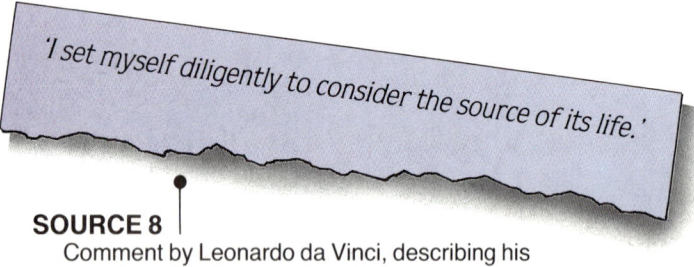

'I set myself diligently to consider the source of its life.'

SOURCE 8
Comment by Leonardo da Vinci, describing his experiments with a growing plant.

SOURCE 9
'The Madonna of the Meadow', a painting by Giovanni Bellini (c 1435–1516). It shows the Virgin Mary holding baby Jesus.

Discovering nature

In the Renaissance, all this changed. As part of their aim to portray reality, artists and scholars made detailed investigations of many kinds of plants and animals. They recorded their findings carefully, in words and pictures. Extracts from two early 16th century notebooks are shown in Sources 7 and 8. Curiosity about the natural world led artists like Leonardo da Vinci to combine several careers (as we would call them today); he was an artist, scientist, inventor and engineer.

This new approach to nature was reflected in many Renaissance paintings. Source 9 is a religious painting, but it is also an accurate picture of a natural landscape. Trees, fields, mother and child are all painted with love and care. Turn back to Source 19 on page 14. See how different medieval and Renaissance treatments of a similar religious theme could be.

Source 10 shows two sketches made by the Renaissance artist Raphael. They are part of his preparations for a painting commissioned by a rich patron. For Raphael, there was no conflict between science and religion. He has studied nature (in this case, a human skeleton) to try and make his finished picture as realistic as possible. He has used this realism to increase the power of the religious message of his painting.

SOURCE 10
Two drawings by Raphael, made in preparation for a larger oil painting which was completed in 1507.

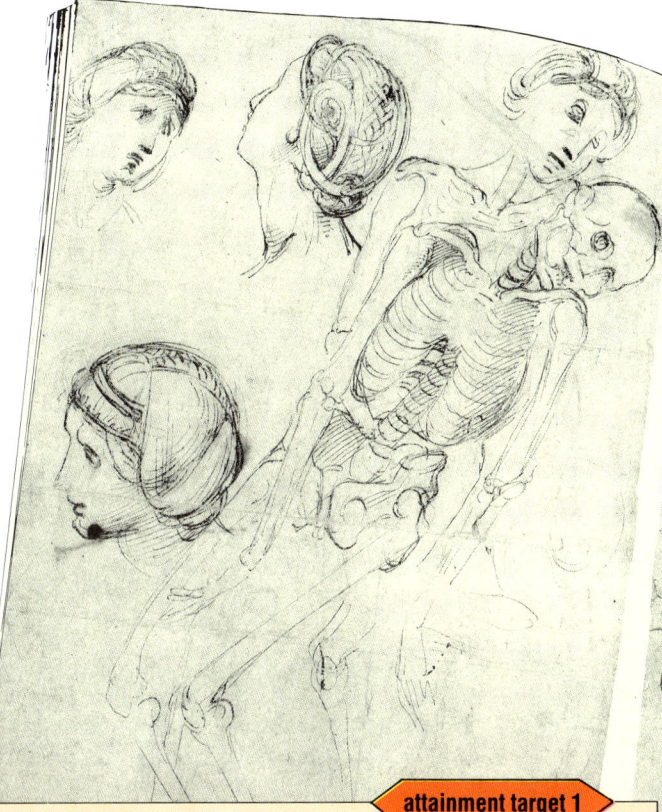

attainment target 1

1 Compare Sources 4 and 5. What changes have taken place in the styles of each of these paintings?

2 Compare Source 9 with Source 19, page 14. What has changed and what has remained the same in the style of these two paintings?

3 Look at Sources 6, 7, 9 and 10. Describe how they illustrate the changes brought about by the Renaissance in showing **perspective**, **nature** and **people** in art of all kinds.

A REBIRTH OF ART

Investigating the past

We have seen that Renaissance artists, scientists and scholars were eager to find out more about the world around them. They were also enthusiastic explorers of the past. Throughout Italy they discovered the remains of buildings and sculptures which had survived from ancient Rome (see Source 11). They also travelled abroad, especially to Greece, to search for traces of the great civilisation that had once existed there.

Whenever they could, they took measurements and made detailed drawings of what interested them. Later, these drawings were copied and sent to scholars all over Europe. In this way, more and more people shared the information about the Greek and Roman past. Source 12 shows one of these scholarly drawings.

SOURCE 11
A TRIUMPHAL ARCH in the city of Rome, built to commemorate the victories of the Emperor Constantine (who ruled AD 306–337).

SOURCE 12
Renaissance artists visited Greece to study the ancient buildings there. These drawings were copied and collected together for use by other scholars. This 15th century drawing of the Parthenon (Athens) was made by Ciriaco d'Ancona.

Writings from ancient times

Renaissance scholars were also keen to find out about the poets, scientists and philosophers of ancient times. Copies of some of their writings had survived, preserved in churches and monasteries. The Italian poet Petrarch, who lived in the late 14th century, was one of the first to go hunting for ancient books and manuscripts. Source 13 reveals his pleasure and excitement on reading, for the first time, the writings of the Roman author Cicero.

As the 15th century progressed, scholars grew more knowledgeable about the Greeks and Romans. They tried to imagine what life had been like in ancient times. They produced poems, plays and paintings in imitation of Greek and Roman styles. Their historical detective work produced a vast store of information about Greek and Roman clothes, weapons, buildings, customs and beliefs. Source 14 shows how one painter, Andrea Mantegna, used this historical information in a painting.

The Renaissance was not only a revolution in art, it also gave new life to many old Greek and Roman subjects and artistic styles.

> Francesco to his Cicero, greetings. Having found your letters where I least expected to, after searching long and hard, I read them avidly [eagerly]. . . . I now at last have come to know yourself. . . .

SOURCE 13
Letter written by the 14th century poet and scholar Francesco Petrarch to the Roman writer and statesman Marcus Tullius Cicero. Cicero died in 43 BC, almost 1400 years before this letter was written.

1. Look at Source 13. Why do you think Petrarch composed a letter to a Roman writer who had been dead for 1400 years? Think of at least two reasons.

2. If you could send a letter to someone living in Renaissance Italy, who would you choose to write to? What questions would you want to ask them? What would you want to say to them about their life and work?

SOURCE 14
Painting by Andrea Mantegna, 'St James on his way to martyrdom', completed around 1450.

A REBIRTH OF ART

Learning from history

For Renaissance artists and scholars, the study of history had a special purpose. They hoped to learn from the past, in order to improve their own world. For them, the ideas and artistic achievements of the Greeks and Romans were better than anything produced since that time. They invented the term 'Middle Ages' to describe the period between the end of the Roman Empire and the beginning of Renaissance times. During those centuries (roughly AD 500–1400), they felt civilisation had declined. Renaissance scholars admired the old Greek and Roman ideals of pride, honour, individual freedom and human dignity. They felt these had been swept away by BARBARIAN invasions and by the teachings of the Christian Church.

This was not altogether true. Many Greek and Roman ideas had survived in Italian city laws and in the organisation of the Church. Even so, philosophers, poets, artists, historians, architects and lawyers in Renaissance Italy looked back longingly to what they believed to be the 'GOLDEN AGE' of ancient Greece and Rome.

This Renaissance interest in the ancient world had some surprising results. Look at Sources 15 and 16. Source 15 shows a Greek temple, built in the 5th century BC. Source 16 shows a Renaissance church, built in the mid-15th century. Designed as a place where Christian men and women could worship, it was decorated in a pagan (non-Christian) style. Houses for wealthy, fashionable people were also built to look like Greek or Roman temples. Source 17 illustrates a SHOWPIECE house, designed by the architect Scamozzi for his family.

SOURCE 15
A typical Greek temple – the Parthenon in Athens, built in the 5th century BC.

SOURCE 16
The church of Sant' Andrea in Mantua, Italy, designed by the architect Alberti around 1460.

Reading history

Books about the past also became very popular during the Renaissance. Even the title of the book quoted in Source 18 tells us something about Renaissance scholars' attitudes to the past. They were humble and respectful. The author of Source 18 obviously expected that his readers would learn useful lessons from history. In Source 19 Niccolò Machiavelli argues that the rulers of 15th and early 16th century Italy were less successful than the great statesmen of the past. He also seems to assume that his readers will agree with him.

SOURCE 17
A villa, or country house, in Roman style – the Rocca Pisani, near Vicenza, Italy, built for his own use by the architect Scamozzi in 1576.

'I award the first place to History, on grounds both of its attractiveness and usefulness, qualities which appeal both to the scholar and the statesman. . . .'

SOURCE 18
From Pier Paulo Vergerio's *De illustribus moribus* (*About the famous dead*), written in Italy in the 15th century.

> If the deeds of our princes are not worth studying for their bravery and dignity, as were those of our ANCESTORS, yet they have other qualities which are no less worth considering . . . one will see with what deceit and with what craft and guile the princes . . . have achieved for themselves a reputation they have never deserved.

SOURCE 19
Written by the Italian historian and political thinker Niccolò Machiavelli during the early 16th century.

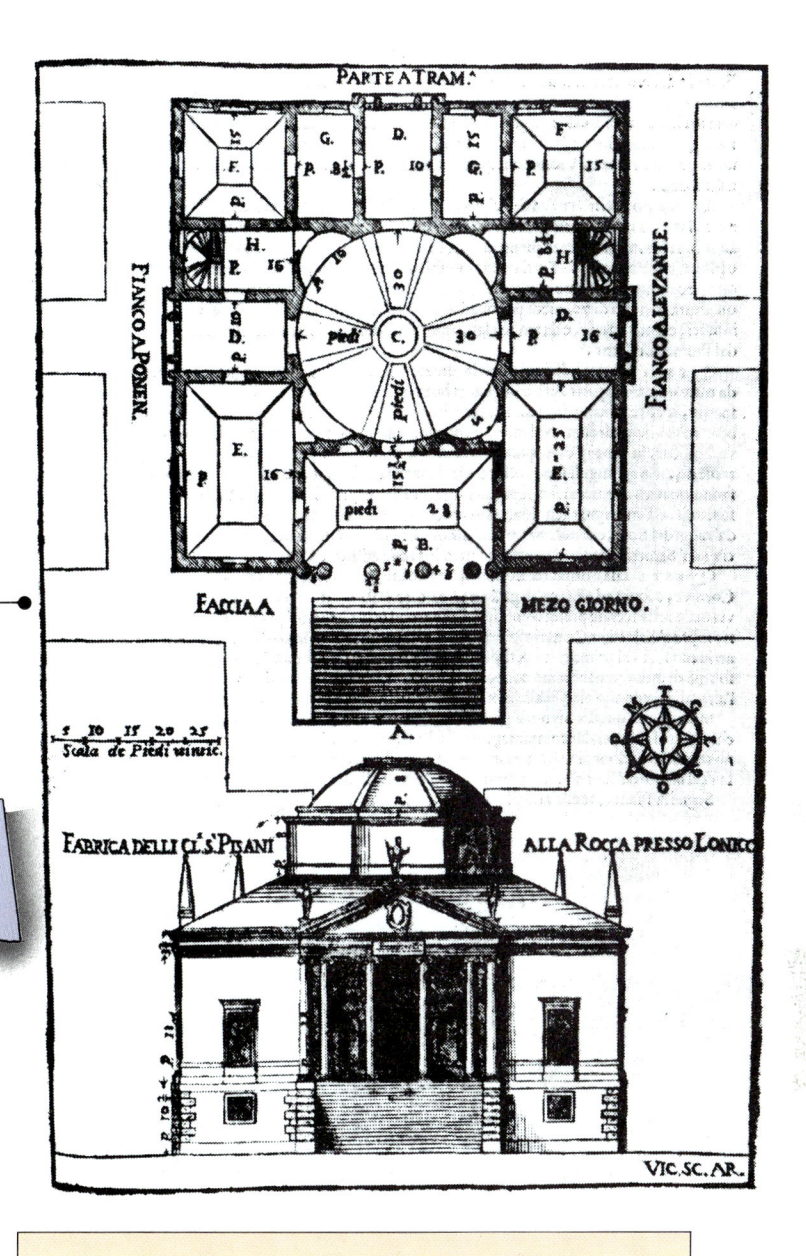

1. Compare Sources 15 and 16. List at least three ways in which the architect Alberti, who built the church shown in Source 16, has copied the Greek temple.

2. If you were a 16th century Italian, would you like to live in the house shown in Source 17? Write two sentences: one suggesting the advantages of living there; the other suggesting the possible disadvantages. You might find Source 10 on page 20 helpful here.

3. Work with a small group to discuss whether you think we can learn anything from history. Make one list of ways in which we might learn, and another containing reasons why we might *not* learn. What is the balance of opinion in your group? What are the views of the class as a whole?

A REBIRTH OF ART

The search for beauty

One of the most important beliefs that Renaissance thinkers borrowed from the past was a respect for human beauty. For the ancient Greeks, a beautiful body was seen as a gift from the gods. Greek artists (especially sculptors) made many statues and carvings of athletes, soldiers and dancers, who were admired for their fitness, strength and grace. The ancient Romans shared this respect for beauty, and their artists produced many fine works celebrating the good looks of men and women of their time.

Both the Greeks and Romans believed that beauty should be more than skin deep. They felt that a beautiful body should house a noble spirit and an intelligent mind. Of course, this was not always the case. But whenever the Greeks or Romans made statues or paintings of their gods and goddesses, they portrayed them as the most beautiful human beings they could imagine.

SOURCE 20
This Greek carving was made in the 4th century BC. It shows Aphrodite, the goddess of love, emerging from the sea. Greek legends described Aphrodite as being 'born from the waves'.

'This maiden, who had lived when Rome flourished, was as shapely as she was noble.'

SOURCE 21
A Renaissance version of the scene shown in Source 20. This picture was painted by the Florentine artist Botticelli around 1485.

SOURCE 22
Comment made by a Renaissance scholar who went to see the remains of an embalmed Roman corpse, discovered by accident in 1485.

Rediscovery

During the medieval period, Church leaders had disapproved of these ideas about physical beauty. In Renaissance Italy, they were rediscovered with delight. Painters and sculptors studied ancient works of art, such as the carving shown in Source 20. They were inspired by them to produce their own statues and paintings of human beauty. Wealthy patrons enjoyed looking at, and owning, these beautiful works of art. Sometimes they shared the artists' philosophical approach to beauty; at other times they just admired the finished product. Source 21, for example, was probably painted to decorate the marriage chamber of a member of the wealthy Medici family in Florence.

The enthusiasm of Renaissance thinkers for studying the past sometimes led them to hold BIASED views about what it had been like. These glowing visions of the past were encouraged when, by chance, the EMBALMED CORPSE of a young (and very beautiful) Roman noblewoman was dug up. Source 22 tells us how one scholar greeted this discovery.

Life for Renaissance women

For women living in Renaissance Italy, everyday life was not so noble or so beautiful. Ordinary women worked hard keeping house, rearing children, cooking, cleaning, caring for sick relatives and helping their husbands with their work. Wealthy women led more comfortable lives, but even they were not free to live as they chose. (Source 23 makes this very clear!) Marriage was their 'career'. It was arranged for them by their families, often to gain social, political or financial benefits, and with little consideration for the woman's feelings. We know the names of several women scholars who lived during the Renaissance. However, as Source 24 makes clear, their careers and achievements were not possible for most women.

Source 25 shows a portrait of one famous Renaissance noblewoman, Lucrezia Borgia. For many years, she had a reputation as an evil, scheming woman. She was thought to have poisoned her friends and enemies, to get her own way. Historians now think that Lucrezia was criticised like this as a way of bringing disgrace on her powerful father and brothers. For most of her adult life, Lucrezia lived quietly at home, acting as adviser to her husband and rearing at least seven children.

SOURCE 25
Portrait medallion of Lucrezia Borgia, who lived from 1480 to 1519.

'It's no use being born a woman if you wish to do what you want.'

SOURCE 23
Comment by Nannina de' Medici, sister of Lorenzo 'The Magnificent', after a disagreement with her husband about how their children should be educated.

... the classical revival did nothing to encourage greater equality for women, quite the reverse. The few successful women scholars are famous just because they were exceptions. ...

SOURCE 24
Comment by a modern historian about Renaissance women.

attainment target 3

1. What can you tell about the position of women in Renaissance Italy from Sources 21–25?

2. What does Source 22 tell us about Renaissance attitudes to Roman women?

3. Source 23 was written at the time; Source 24 was written by a modern historian. How far do they agree with each other? How useful is each of them in finding out about women in the Renaissance?

4. What would you want to know about Source 24 before deciding how reliable it was?

5. Is Source 25 any help to us in deciding whether or not Lucrezia Borgia was wicked? Explain your answer.

A REBIRTH OF ART

Human values

During the MIDDLE AGES, the Christian Church had encouraged people to live their lives 'with a view to ETERNITY'. That is, to behave as if all their thoughts and actions would one day be judged by God. According to the Church, everyone was sinful in one way or another – it was part of being human. No man or woman was perfect, but everyone had a duty to behave well.

The growth of humanism

We have already seen how Renaissance artists and philosophers welcomed the rediscovery of ancient ideas about beauty – of mind, body and spirit. These ideas led on to a new philosophy, known as humanism, which challenged the teachings of the medieval Church. Renaissance thinkers made human beings, and human achievements, their main concern. They cared more about life in this world, than about eternity. You can see some examples of ancient and humanist ideas in Source 26. Most humanists did not reject God altogether. But now they believed that, in some ways, humans could be perfect, and almost equal to God.

SOURCE 27
Drawing by Leonardo da Vinci, made between 1485 and 1490, to illustrate the theories of Vitruvius, a Roman architect.

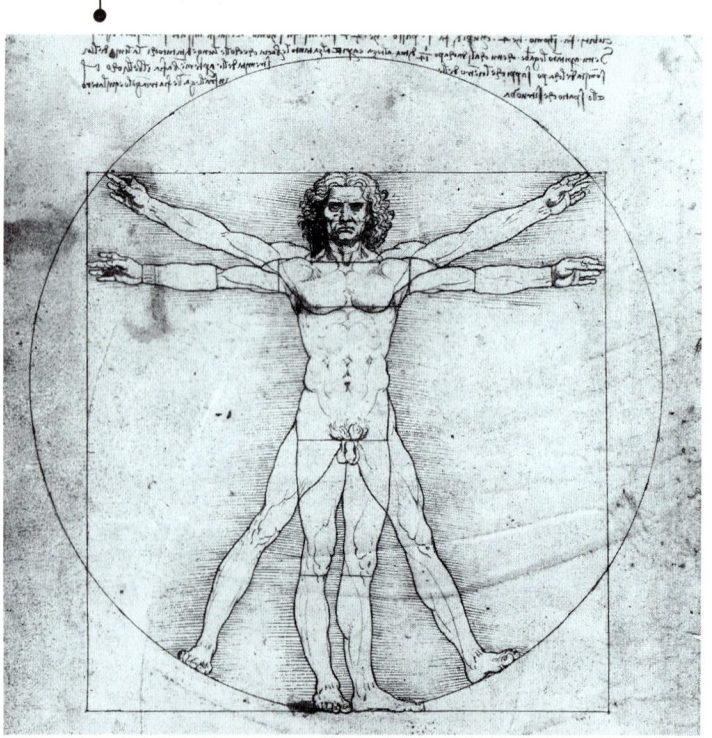

'I am a man. Nothing human is alien to me.'
'Men can do all things if they will.'
'Man is the measure of all things.'

SOURCE 26
Sayings by (from the top): Roman poet Terence (195–159 BC); Renaissance scholar and artist Leon Battista Alberti (1404–1472); and Greek philosopher Protagoros, who lived in the 5th century BC.

The divine pattern

The discoveries made by Renaissance scholars in subjects as different as ANATOMY, music and maths all helped the humanists. Scholars considered certain shapes, such as squares and circles, to be mathematically perfect. They were delighted that Roman architect Vitruvius had suggested that a perfect human body was naturally in HARMONY with these perfect mathematical forms. (You can see a Renaissance illustration of this idea in Source 27.) They took this harmony as evidence of a 'grand design', by which the universe had been formed. God, the 'great architect', had created humanity as part of a beautiful, perfect pattern. Artists believed it was their duty to understand this pattern, and try to reproduce it in their own work.

Source 28 shows one of the frescos made by the artist Michaelangelo to decorate a chapel belonging to the Pope in Rome. It is a magnificent study of the human body. But Michaelangelo intended his painting to be more than just a picture: it is a statement of humanist beliefs in the power and beauty of humankind. Adam, described in the Bible as the first human being, is being awakened with the 'spark of life' by God. Michaelangelo believed that without God, Adam could not live. Even so, he has portrayed him as strong, relaxed and unafraid.

Michaelangelo's painting shows us that, for some Renaissance artists, humanity could be almost divine (Godlike). Other painters and sculptors were interested in studying humanity for its own sake. They produced 'PSYCHOLOGICAL' portraits of individual men and women (such as the one shown in Source 29). These works portray the sitter's inner character as well as their outward appearance. They go deeper than the mere images of wealth and power, which were usual in earlier portraits.

A REBIRTH OF ART

SOURCE 29
Portrait of a woman, known as the 'Mona Lisa', painted by Leonardo da Vinci around 1502.

SOURCE 28
God giving life to Adam (according to the Bible, the first man on earth), from a series of paintings in the Sistine Chapel, Rome, made by Michaelangelo between 1508 and 1512.

ACTIVITY

1. Look at Source 29, Leonardo da Vinci's painting of the Italian noblewoman. It is one of the most famous portraits in the world. Can you suggest why it has fascinated people for nearly 500 years? Discuss this with other members of your class.

2. Now write a sentence describing Leonardo's artistic technique; for example, how he has used colour, misty shadows and light, to create an interesting picture.

3. 'Mona Lisa' was a real woman. Compare her with the picture of the female servant picking cherries in Source 21 on page 15. How are the two women shown differently? Think of at least two words to describe this difference.

4. Now look at the picture of Battista Sforza (Source 6 on page 18). She, too, was a real woman, but her portrait looks very different from Mona Lisa's. How has Leonardo da Vinci managed to show something 'extra' about Mona Lisa in his picture?

5. It is a matter of individual taste whether we like a picture (by any artist, past or present), or not. Write a sentence which begins *either* 'I like Leonardo's painting of the Mona Lisa because . . .' *or* 'I don't like Leonardo's painting of the Mona Lisa because . . .'.

A REBIRTH OF ART

Humanist learning

Renaissance artists' interest in people was shared by writers of the time. They studied the works of Greek and Roman authors not only to find out about the past (as we saw on pages 34–35), but also out of curiosity. As one Renaissance thinker put it, ancient texts 'were full of SPECULATION about the nature of things'. What was the world really like? What kind of a creature was man/woman? What made people act the way they did? Was it love? hate? greed? fear? the hope of riches? or respect for the community and its laws?

To help them understand these ancient texts, Renaissance scholars studied the old Greek and Latin languages, helped by professors from distant lands. They prepared new versions of old manuscripts (see Source 30) and established strict rules for spelling, handwriting and grammar. The invention of printing in Germany in the mid-15th century gave a boost to this process of learning, writing and publishing. Scholarly rulers, such as Federico da Montefeltro (Source 31), spent money on new libraries to house their rapidly growing collections of books and manuscripts.

SOURCE 30
Engraving by Enea Vico (c 1550), after an earlier work by Baccio Bandinelli. It shows Bandinelli's academy for artists, established in 1531.

attainment target 2

1 Look back at the paintings, buildings and sculptures shown so far in this unit. Choose two of them which you think are good examples of the new Renaissance style. Write down their Source numbers. Copy out this sentence, and add your own words to complete it: 'Source _____ and Source _____ are typical Renaissance works of art because _____.'

2 Now compare your choice of Sources, and your completed sentence, with the answers given by the rest of your class. Work together to make a list to answer the question: 'What makes a work of art typically Renaissance in style and content?'

SOURCE 31
Federico da Montefeltro and his young son – painting probably by Pedro Berruguete, completed about 1477.

From craftsman to celebrity

Renaissance artists, writers and scholars also found a new ROLE for themselves. Source 32 shows a scene in an early 15th century workshop. Craftsmen are working together as a team, to produce paintings and sculptures. This was the way in which most artists worked in the centuries before the Renaissance. Painters and sculptors trained by working alongside a master craftsman. They did the simple tasks, while he concentrated on the difficult sections of a work – painting the face, perhaps, or carving the hands. Eventually, the trainees set up workshops of their own, and became masters. Many medieval artists were anonymous; they did not sign their work and their names have not survived.

During the Renaissance, all this changed. Painters and sculptors continued to train together in workshops, but top artists now became famous as individuals. They were greeted by kings, popes and princes as honoured guests, and treated almost as equals. Their views were listened to, their tastes admired and their finished paintings and sculptures eagerly bought. As Source 33 shows, they now signed their names proudly on their canvases, and sometimes included portraits of themselves in their work. Very famous artists, such as Michaelangelo, developed a strong sense of their own importance. He was deeply insulted (as Source 34 on page 44 shows) by being treated like an ordinary craft worker.

Source 35 is an example of the extravagant praise heaped on one of the most celebrated Renaissance artists, Tiziano Vecellio (usually known as 'Titian'). He was reported to be an intelligent, friendly and generous man. Most historians agree that he was a brilliant painter. (You can see his thoughtful self-portrait in Source 36.) Yet it is hard to believe he was the greatest man in 16th century Europe, as his friend's remark implies.

SOURCE 32
Carving showing scene in a sculptor's workshop, made by Nanni di Banco about 1408.

SOURCE 33
Detail from a painting, completed in 1459, by Benozzo Gozzoli. The artist has painted himself as an onlooker to the main scene. He has written 'Opus Benotii' ('Benozzo's work') round his hat. The full painting is on page 23.

A REBIRTH OF ART

Highly praised

Even if we think it is ridiculous, Source 35 reminds us that some artists in Renaissance Italy were highly praised. Why was this? How did the change from craftsman to celebrity come about? Partly, the revolutionary changes in style had made art (and artists) more noticeable. People now expected paintings and buildings to shock or surprise. It was partly because wealthy patrons competed with one another to attract brilliant scholars, philosophers and artists to their courts. They wanted to demonstrate their own good taste and learning, and to share in their guests' glory. Also, the humanists' new view of the world suggested a different way of looking at artists, writers and musicians. They were no longer just craft workers; they shared in the Godlike process of creation, as well.

> Tell him not to address his letters to "the sculptor Michaelangelo", for here I am only known as Michaelangelo Buonarotti.... I have never been a painter or a sculptor, in the sense of having kept a shop....

SOURCE 34
Complaint made by Michaelangelo Buonarotti.

> 'The first man in CHRISTENDOM.'

SOURCE 35
Description of the Venetian artist Titian by one of his friends.

Some Renaissance 'celebrities'

Donatello (1386–1456)
Sculptor. Born in Florence. Helped to develop new theories of perspective. Interested in Greek and Roman antiquities. Trained with Ghiberti and helped to make the great bronze doors of Florence Cathedral (Source 14, page 21). Produced many sculptures for patrons in Florence, including the Medici family, and in other Italian cities. His style was bold and dramatic.

'Titian' – Tiziano Vecellio (c 1490–1576)
Painter. Born in north Italy and travelled to Venice (aged 9), to study with the Bellini family. Then he worked as an assistant to other Venetian painters. Worked on frescos as well as smaller paintings. Interested in Greek and Roman stories, and used them to provide subjects for his paintings. Also painted fine portraits and religious pictures, and many beautiful nudes. His work was admired for its SUMPTUOUS use of colour, elegance and psychological awareness (see Source 36). Became famous throughout Europe. Made a nobleman by the Holy Roman Emperor, because he was so pleased with Titian's portrait of him.

SOURCE 36
Self-portrait by Titian, painted in 1562.

Tomasso Masaccio (1401–1428)
Painter. Went to live in Florence aged 16. Experimented with new techniques of realism (Source 2, page 29). Interested in humanism and tried to reflect this in his paintings. Died very young (aged 27) but his few completed works influenced many later artists. One of the founders of the Renaissance in Florence.

Leonardo da Vinci (1452–1519)

Painter, scientist, inventor, engineer. Came to live in Florence as a young man. Trained with famous Florentine artists; much admired for his skill at drawing. Interested in mathematics; tried to design his pictures according to his mathematical theories of perfect shapes. Famous also for his skill at psychological portraits, and for the mystery with which he surrounded his figures (e.g. Source 29, page 41). He used the same 'shadowy' techniques in his religious paintings, to inspire awe and reverence. Travelled to Milan to work as an engineer for the powerful Sforza DYNASTY: designed bridges, canals, forts, weapons. Experimented with plans for submarines and flying machines. Studied anatomy and made detailed drawings of people, plants and animals. Was also interested in chemistry, optics (science of how we see), architecture, town planning, ASTRONOMY and geography. Became famous and highly respected throughout Italy and elsewhere in Europe, especially in France.

Alessandro Botticelli (1444–1510)

Painter. Born in Florence, from a poor family. Trained as a goldsmith, then with famous Florentine painters. His talent was spotted by the Medici family, who encouraged him. Interested in Greek philosophy; used ancient Greek ideas in his work. Also painted many Christian religious works, and was influenced by Savonarola's preachings (see pages 26–27). His style was elegant and graceful. Most famous works include 'Primavera' (Source 24, page 25) and 'Birth of Venus' (Source 21, page 38).

Giovanni Bellini (c 1430–1516)

Painter. Born in Venice. Member of well-known family of artists. Trained in his father's workshop. Skilled at delicate drawing. Also famous for his ability to portray light and colour. His paintings show his keen awareness of the natural world (e.g. Source 9, page 32). Developed new techniques for painting, using oil-based paints – a Renaissance invention. Helped to make his home city of Venice a major centre of Renaissance art by training many important painters in his workshop.

Michaelangelo Buonarotti (1475–1564)

Painter, sculptor, poet and architect. Aged 13, travelled to Florence and worked with many leading Florentine artists, including Donatello. Invited to live in the Medici palace by Lorenzo 'The Magnificent'. Met many scholars and poets there, and became interested in philosophy and the ancient world. His work is powerful, noble, original and sometimes startling. Many of his best works (e.g. Source 28, page 41) are studies of the human figure. He wanted to portray the spiritual qualities of his subjects, as well as their physical beauty. Other major works deal with religious themes, and powerfully express grief, pain and suffering (see Source 12, page 55). His poems reveal his own passionate (and sometimes TORMENTED) feelings, about life, love, art and religion. Travelled to Rome to work on a number of projects for the popes, including the Sistine Chapel. Returned to Florence to work on a series of Medici tombs, but was summoned back to Rome. Continued to work on religious sculpture until a week before his death, aged 89.

SOURCE 37
Self-portrait by Leonardo da Vinci, painted in about 1512.

ACTIVITY

1. Imagine that you were young Titian sent to an artist's workshop (like the one on page 43) at the age of 9. How would you feel, alone in the big city? What would your hopes and ambitions be? Would you be nervous or frightened? Write a letter to your parents describing your feelings at the end of your first week away from home.

2. Look at the 'mini biographies' of Renaissance artists on these pages. How were their lives similar, and how were they different? Write and illustrate a 'timeline' (see page 5) to show all the stages in the life of a successful Renaissance artist.

A REBIRTH OF ART

Science and discovery

Renaissance scholars believed that it was possible for human beings to discover most things by using their God-given intelligence. Source 38 quotes part of an imaginary dialogue between God and Adam, written by Pico della Mirandola, which explains this. Renaissance thinkers were confident of their power to make new discoveries in scientific activities like building and engineering, as well as the arts. Source 39 shows a sketch by Michaelangelo; it shows how he searched for the figure he believed to be 'hidden' in a block of marble. Unlike many modern artists, Michaelangelo did not look for materials to make something already worked out on paper. Instead, he 'explored' each lump of stone to discover the possible statues it contained.

New techniques for new buildings

Renaissance architects and builders shared this spirit of experiment and discovery. They copied old styles of building, dating from Greek and Roman times. But they also invented many daring new techniques to make bigger and grander buildings than anything seen in ancient times. The dome of Florence Cathedral, illustrated in Source 40, was one of the earliest Renaissance building projects. Its architect, Brunelleschi, used his knowledge of an ancient Roman building, the Pantheon in Rome. He built a vast structure covering an open space 43 metres wide. This would have been impossible using medieval building technology. Brunelleschi managed it by copying and improving upon an ancient design.

Later designers, like Leonardo da Vinci, went further. He made astounding new inventions, such as the primitive helicopter shown in Source 41. Leonardo's machine was never built but its design shows the confidence and bravery of Renaissance engineers.

SOURCE 39
Sketch by Michaelangelo, 'Sea God still embedded in the marble', made between 1520–1525.

Filippo Brunelleschi (1377–1466)
Architect. Trained as a goldsmith, but left this work and travelled to Rome to study ancient buildings. Returned to Florence to work on the Cathedral dome, the Innocenti Hospital, churches, chapels and many other buildings.

Leon Battista Alberti (1404–1472)
Architect and humanist scholar. Born into a wealthy Florentine family; exiled for political reasons but later returned to Florence. Studied law, but became friends with many famous Florentine artists. Wrote a book about the 'new' Renaissance style of painting, and a textbook on architecture. Studied Vitruvius and other architects. Designed many buildings, including grand houses and churches in the Roman temple style. Also wrote poetry, a book on grammar, and books about family life.

Donato Bramante (c 1444–1514)
Architect. Trained as a painter. Interested in Greek and Roman architectural styles. Influenced by Brunelleschi's work. Worked for the Sforza family in Milan, and later in Rome, designing churches, chapels, fine houses and monuments. Worked on new designs for St Peter's Church in Rome. Although many of his designs were later abandoned, they influenced other Renaissance architects for years to come.

'God said to Adam, "I have placed you in the centre of the world, so that you may more easily see and discover all that it contains . . ."'

SOURCE 38
From a speech by philosopher Giovanni Pico della Mirandola (1463–1494) on 'The Dignity of Man'.

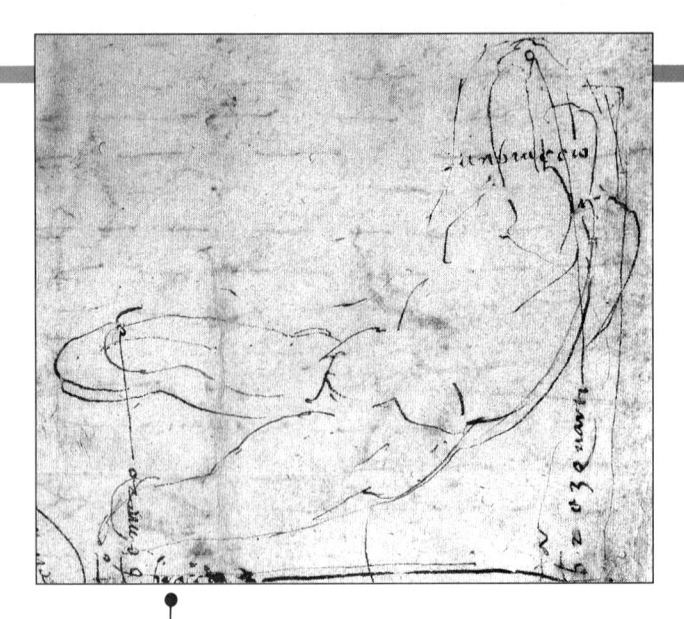

A REBIRTH OF ART

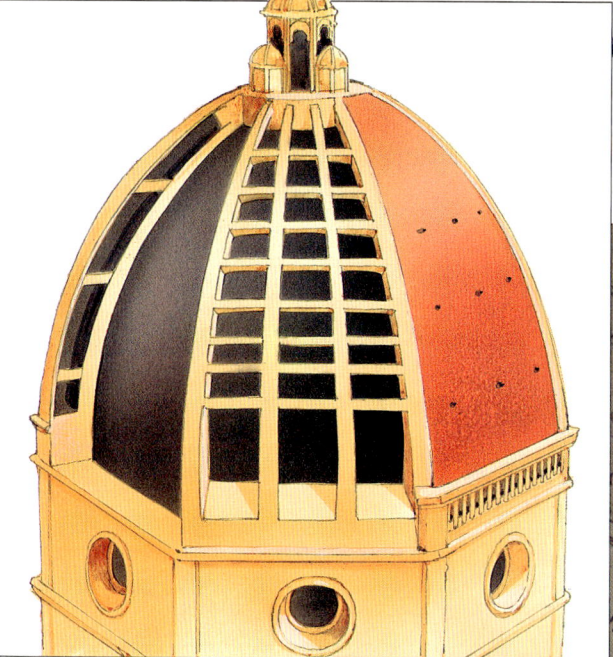

SOURCE 40
Section through the dome of Florence Cathedral, designed by Brunelleschi in 1420.

SOURCE 41
One of Leonardo da Vinci's inventions – a man-powered helicopter – sketched shortly after 1530.

1. In what ways do Sources 39, 40 and 41 all show that Renaissance people made startling new discoveries?
2. Compare the quotation in Source 38 with the comments by Greek and Renaissance thinkers quoted in Source 26 on page 40. How do they reveal a similar view of humanity's place in the world?
3. Leonardo's helicopter (Source 41) would probably not work. Does this mean this source is of no interest to us?

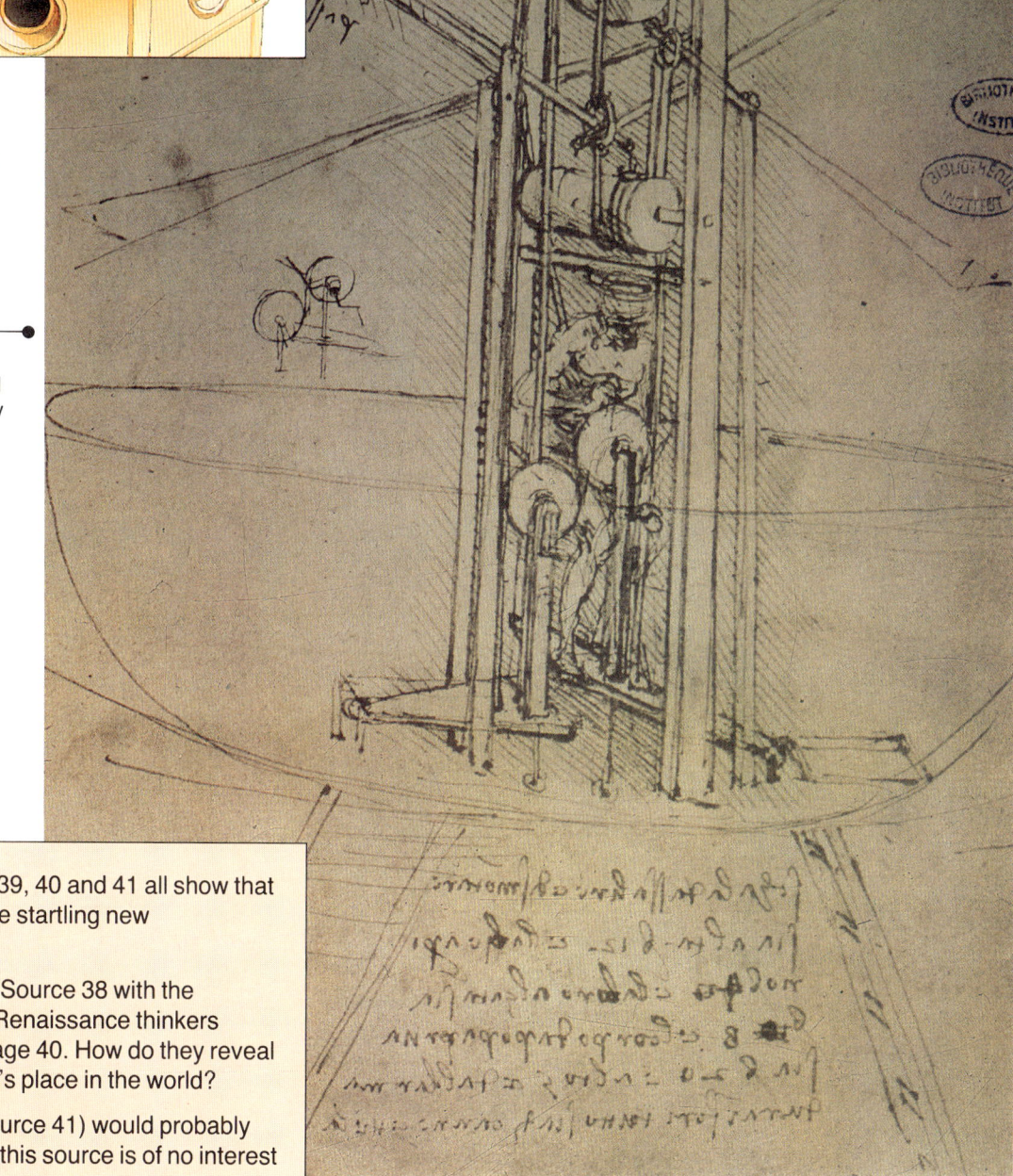

A REBIRTH OF ART

Exploring the universe

Renaissance confidence and curiosity did not stop with exploring the Greek and Roman past, or constructing daring new buildings in Italy. All over Europe, scholars and adventurers made plans to explore the rest of the world, and the heavens beyond. Prince Henry the Navigator of Portugal founded a college for would-be explorers, and collected a magnificent library of geography books. Encouraged by patrons like Prince Henry, sailors, adventurers and scientists made preparations to set sail and discover what lay in the lands beyond the horizon.

Sailing the seas

The Italian explorer Christopher Columbus is probably the most famous of these Renaissance navigators; but there were many others. All who survived their voyages brought back useful new information. This was collected together and published in books, such as the example illustrated in Source 42. Stay-at-home geographers also played their part in this rush to explore the globe. They made accurate, detailed maps (see Source 43), which helped explorers find their way in unknown territory.

SOURCE 42
Drawing of the structure of the universe, with the planets circling round the Sun, used to illustrate the works of Tycho Brahe, a Danish Renaissance astronomer.

SOURCE 43
Map of the world, drawn about 1489 by the German map-maker Henricus Martellus, who lived and worked in Florence. It shows the newly discovered sea route round the southern tip of Africa.

A REBIRTH OF ART

'It is a universal condition of men to want to know.'

SOURCE 44
Comment by the Spanish explorer, Hernan Cortes (1485–1547).

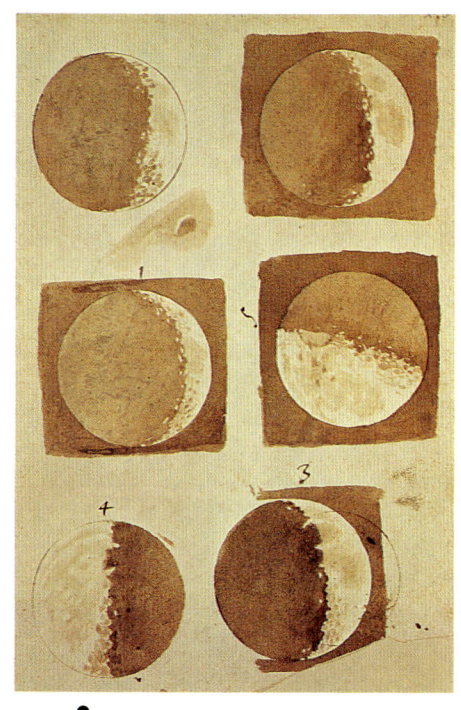

SOURCE 45
Sketches made by Galileo, after he had studied the moon through one of the first ever telescopes, 1609–1610.

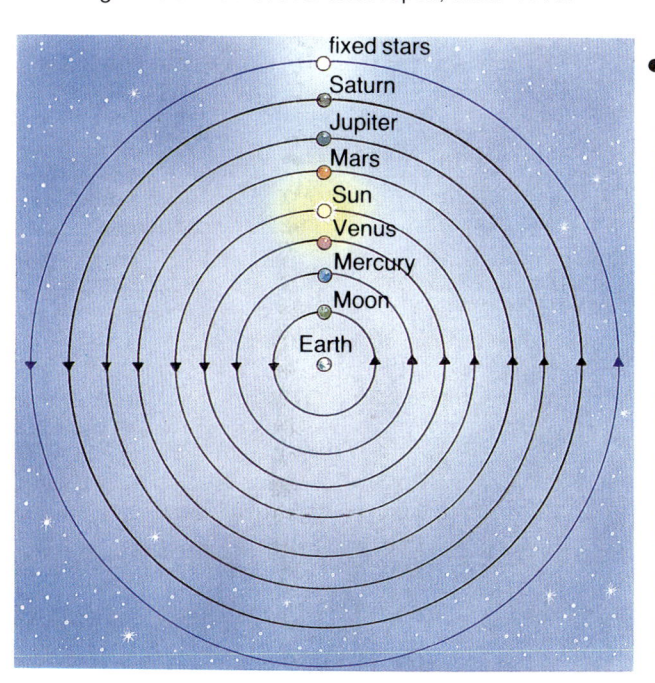

SOURCE 46
The solar system as described by a medieval astronomer. Copernicus disproved this theory.

Observing the stars

Explorers like Cortes, quoted in Source 44, shared the Renaissance belief that the thirst for new knowledge was part of human nature. Cortes was an active traveller, but other explorers spent their time indoors in observatories, studying the heavens. They were dissatisfied with medieval views of space, which placed the earth at the centre of the universe. They made observations of the movements of the Sun, moon and stars. By their calculations, they proved that the medieval view was wrong. Scientists like the Polish mathematician Copernicus and the Italian astronomer Galileo suggested that the Earth and the nearby planets revolve around the Sun (see Source 45). Modern science agrees with this view, but it shocked the Church authorities because it seemed disrespectful to God. You can see how Renaissance opinions about the position of our world in the universe differed from medieval views by looking at Source 46.

A new view of creation

The discoveries made by Renaissance scientists soon became known among scholars and thinkers all over Europe. Instead of provoking a contempt for God and His creation, as the Church had feared, they inspired a new respect for all the marvels of nature.

ACTIVITY

Work in a small group. Imagine that you have just come on board a Renaissance explorer's ship, which is getting ready to sail for unknown lands. Some of you are scholars, one is a map-maker, one is an artist, one is an astronomer and the rest are sailors. Why have you chosen to travel? What do you hope to find? Are you excited, curious, frightened, or a mixture of all three? Write a short scene where you all meet on deck. At first, you make polite conversation, but as you lose sight of land you can't help showing your real feelings. Act out the scene in front of other members of the class.

UNIT 4

Renaissance heritage

The Renaissance did not happen in Italy alone. Italian artists, architects, philosophers and writers were all helped and encouraged by colleagues in northern and southern Europe.

The northern Renaissance

Renaissance artists learned new styles and skills from painters living and working in Germany and the Netherlands. Source 1 shows a double portrait of a wealthy Italian couple, painted while they were staying in the city of Bruges (in present-day Belgium). The artist, Jan van Eyck, was famous for his skill at realistic portraits. As you can see, he has created a picture which is almost as clear and sharp as a modern photograph. He has also used some clever tricks to add extra interest to his work. There is a round mirror on the back wall of the room, in which the artist himself is reflected, paintbrush in hand. He has also signed 'Jan Eyck was here' (in Latin) on the wall above the mirror. In contrast, Source 2 shows a delicate self-portrait by the German artist, Albrecht Dürer. We can sense the artist's nervous, precise and thoughtful temperament, reflected in his work. Paintings like these were inspired by many of the same ideals as Italian Renaissance paintings, and taught Italian painters many new techniques.

AIMS

In this unit, we shall look at how Renaissance ideas spread beyond Italy to influence artists and scholars all over Europe. We shall also discuss whether the Renaissance was or was not a 'turning point', as many historians have claimed. Finally, we shall look at the Renaissance heritage – how Renaissance ideas have continued to play a part in western civilisation for many hundreds of years.

SOURCE 2
Self-portrait by the German artist Albrecht Dürer (1471–1528), painted 1498.

SOURCE 1
'The Marriage of Giovanni Arnolfini and Giovanna Cenami', a painting by the Netherlands artist Jan van Eyck, dated 1434.

Poets and scholars

Northern Europe was also home to many famous Renaissance scholars. They were particularly skilful at studying and editing ancient texts.

The Netherlands scholar, Erasmus of Rotterdam (? 1469–1536) made a vast collection of important quotations from ancient Greek and Roman authors, which he called his 'Adages'. During a visit to Italy in 1508, Erasmus arranged for these Adages (now numbering 3,000) to be printed. The books proved so bulky that he had to hire an extra horse to carry them back to Rotterdam. Erasmus worked closely with other learned colleagues, in England, France and Germany.

Renaissance ideas were soon included in northern European literature. In England, poets and playwrights like Marlowe, Spenser and Shakespeare used many Renaissance ideas in their work. Source 3 shows how the new Renaissance ideas of human dignity were expressed in English works. Source 4 shows how Renaissance styles of architecture were applied in England.

1. In what ways is Source 1 like Italian Renaissance paintings? In what ways is it different?
2. Renaissance scholars (such as Erasmus of Rotterdam) wanted to improve education. From what you have read so far in this book, can you suggest what subjects they wanted their pupils to study?
3. Look at the two quotations in Source 3. Make a list, in your own words, of the qualities which the speaker in Shakespeare's play admired in human beings. Are these typically Renaissance qualities?

'O brave new world . . .'

'What a piece of work is man, how noble in reason, how infinite in faculties, in form and moving, how express and admirable . . . in action, how like an angel, in apprehension, how like a god: the beauty of the world; the paragon of animals. . . .'

infinite in faculties = possessing many skills
express = fast
apprehension = understanding
paragon = best

SOURCE 3
Lines from William Shakespeare's plays *The Tempest* and *Hamlet*. Shakespeare (1564–1616) was the leading dramatist of the English Renaissance.

SOURCE 4
Montacute House in Somerset, started in 1588 and completed in 1601.

RENAISSANCE HERITAGE

France and Spain

France and Spain have always been close to Italy, both geographically and through their common Roman heritage. During the Renaissance, artists and scholars moved freely from one country to another, sharing their ideas and learning with foreign colleagues. Sources 5 and 9 show splendid examples of this. The magnificent CHATEAU of Chambord (Source 5) was designed by an Italian architect, but built by French craftsmen. It contains a mixture of traditional French features, such as the little towers and soaring roofs, and new Italian styles, based on ancient Greek and Roman designs.

Royal and noble patrons

French patrons, especially the kings and their court, encouraged Italian artists to come and work for them. Leonardo da Vinci spent many years working for King François I. French noblewomen, such as Diane de Poitiers (Source 6), spent large sums of money rebuilding and decorating their chateaux in the latest Renaissance styles.

In Spain, too, there was keen interest in Renaissance ideas. Source 7 shows the tomb of a Spanish nobleman, built to a Spanish Renaissance design. It is realistic in style – the statue on the tomb looks very true to life. It also reflects a typical Renaissance, humanist respect for learning: the young nobleman buried beneath the sculpture is shown reading a book. Studying and reading for pleasure were both now admired as worthwhile ways of passing the time. Significantly, there is little room in this tomb memorial for thoughts of God.

SOURCE 5
The Chateau of Chambord, France, designed by the Italian architect Domenico da Cortona, with the assistance of three French master-builders. It was completed in 1547.

SOURCE 6
Diane de Poitiers (1499–1566), mistress of King Henry II of France, and a great patron of painters and architects.

RENAISSANCE HERITAGE

SOURCE 7
Tomb of the Spanish nobleman Martin Vaquez de Arce in Sigüenza, Spain. It was designed by Sebastian de Almonacid and build shortly after 1486.

Humanism – and humour

France and Spain did not rely on Italian 'imports' of Renaissance ideas. They both produced many fine painters, scholars and writers of their own. French and Spanish artists travelled to Italy to win fame and fortune there. The Spanish writer, Cervantes, was admired throughout Europe for his humorous novel describing the adventures of a disaster-prone knight, Don Quixote. Source 8 shows examples of Renaissance poetry written by the French writer Pierre de Ronsard.

'Ronsard me celebroit du temps que j'estois belle.'
('Ronsard praised me, in the days when I was young and beautiful.')

'Cuillez aujourd'hui les roses de la vie.'
('Gather life's roses today.'
[meaning: don't hesitate because life and love will soon pass you by.])

SOURCE 8
Lines (with translations) from poems by the French writer Pierre de Ronsard, who lived about 1424–1585.

SOURCE 9
Spanish pendant, made c 1600. Interest in exotic animals like parrots came about because of the contact between Spain and the 'New World' (Columbus had reached America in 1492).

ACTIVITY

Look again at Source 7. Wealthy people often discussed the design of their own tombs with artists, long before they were dead. Imagine that you were a wealthy noblewoman or man living in Renaissance Europe. What instructions about subject, style and design would you give to the artist/craftsman?

If you were planning your own tomb today, what would you want it to look like? Discuss both questions with other members of your class.

RENAISSANCE HERITAGE

A turning point?

Did the Renaissance really change life in Italy and throughout Europe? It all depends who we are talking about. For ordinary people, many of the dramatic new developments in the Renaissance passed them by. Their lives remained much the same; working, eating, sleeping, caring for their children and living in fear of poverty, death and disease. They certainly could not afford to buy, and probably never even saw, many famous Renaissance works of art. Their closest contact with Renaissance ideas came through the new religious paintings and statues they saw. These were paid for privately by rich patrons but displayed in public, and therefore visible to all.

The cultured classes

When we look at the lives of wealthy people, the picture is different. Their ideas, tastes, ambitions and beliefs did change. By the end of the 15th century, an Italian noble was expected to be well-educated, and knowledgeable about painting, music and all the arts. He (or she) paid for new and beautiful buildings. They were expected to understand Greek and Roman philosophy, and to model their behaviour on brave, stern and ruthless heroes described in histories. Even their Christian faith might be mixed with rediscovered pagan ideas.

SOURCE 10
Typical medieval art: 12th century stone carving of Eve from Autun Cathedral, France.

SOURCE 11
Magnificent Renaissance art: wall painted by Michaelangelo in the Sistine Chapel, Rome. Completed in 1541, it shows a vision based on a passage from the Bible.

The power of art

In the world of art, there had also been many changes in style and in content. Look back at unit 3 if you want to remind yourself what the changes were. Sources 10 and 11 will also help you to do this.

SOURCE 12
Unfinished statue by Michaelangelo, carved 1554–1564. It shows the Virgin Mary supporting the dead Jesus, after he had been crucified.

Beyond technique

But Source 12 shows us that these Renaissance visions of the power and possibilities of art could lead even further. Michaelangelo was eager to explore the deepest, most painful depths of emotion, and to present them to us. To do this he has abandoned his training and technique, and hacked away at the marble to produce a tragic, broken figure. Many people find this shattered image of the dead Jesus even more powerful than the brilliant painting in Source 11. What do you think?

ACTIVITY

Renaissance artists and architects eagerly copied Greek and Roman designs and used the new techniques of realism and perspective to create their works. This gave rise to a typical style which almost all Renaissance artists used. Today, artists and architects work in a variety of styles. If you were an artist would you prefer to live in a time like the Renaissance where there are accepted rules for 'good' art, or today where there is total freedom? Discuss this with other members of your class.

attainment target 1

Imagine that you are *either* a poor citizen *or* a member of a wealthy family like the Medici living in Italy in 1400. By magic carpet you are able to travel forwards in time through a whole century to reach the year 1500. Think about what life all around you will be like then. Now think about and answer these questions.

1 What changes will you see in your daily life?

2 What will have changed most in your surroundings?

3 What will have changed hardly at all?

4 What changes will have affected only certain people?

5 Who will have benefited most from the changes?

6 How do you think Italy as a whole will have been changed?

Now complete this sentence:

'The Renaissance was a turning point because _____.'

Renaissance and Reformation

Renaissance curiosity about the living world encouraged new scientific discoveries in many parts of Europe. Source 13 shows a Renaissance scientist at work. Some of his scientific instruments look old-fashioned to us today (see also Source 14). However, they helped scientists during the Renaissance make many important discoveries, especially in anatomy, chemistry and optics. Perhaps even more important was the fact that Renaissance scientists adopted a new, critical and enquiring outlook in their work. They experimented, studied, observed, asked questions and FORMULATED new theories. They took nothing on trust, not even the teachings of the Church.

This scientific approach spread to the study of historical remains and ancient manuscripts, including the text of the Bible. Some people were scandalised by this, since they regarded the Bible as a holy book and so beyond criticism. But the invention of printing allowed the rapid spread of these new critical attitudes. Books were now quicker, cheaper and easier to produce. Source 15 compares a handwritten manuscript with a book printed in the 15th century.

SOURCE 13
The Renaissance scientist Luca Pacioli in his study, with a pupil; painted by an unknown Italian artist in 1495.

SOURCE 14
Earliest surviving spring-driven clock, made by Jacob Zech in 1525.

SOURCE 15
Left: handwritten manuscript of 1428 copying a Roman text by Cicero.
Right: 1465 book printed using 'italic' type (a style based on Renaissance printers' attempts to copy ancient Roman writing).

Reforming religion

Scientific questioning and the rapid spread of new ideas through printed books were important in another way. Books provided new scholarly information for religious reformers of the late 15th and 16th centuries. These religious protesters called for improvements in Church organisation, and better behaviour by priests, monks and nuns. They also quarrelled with the Church authorities about certain basic Christian teachings. They demanded the right to hold services in the way they felt was best; they wanted the Bible translated from Latin into modern languages. Then everyone could study it, and discuss its teachings for themselves. Source 16 shows the title page of one of the first Bibles to be printed in English.

These religious reformers (who soon became known as Protestants) strongly believed in the right to be guided by their own understanding of the Christian faith and to worship God in their own way. Source 17 records a famous remark made by Martin Luther, the leading German Protestant. He claimed that his conscience forced him to oppose the Pope in Rome. This led to the setting up of a new, reformed church where people seeking similar religious truths could worship.

Artistic experiment, scientific discoveries and CONTROVERSIAL opinions all created an atmosphere of anxiety mingled with excitement in early 16th century Europe. It is not surprising (as Source 17 tells us) that many people felt that the whole of their world was changing.

SOURCE 16
Title page of a printed translation of the Bible, produced in England in 1539, designed by the artist Hans Holbein.

'Here I make my stand. I cannot do otherwise.'

'Wherever I turn, I see things changed. . . .'

SOURCE 17
The first remark is by the German religious reformer, Martin Luther (1483–1546); the second comment is by the Netherlands scholar, Erasmus of Rotterdam.

1. Look at Source 13. How has the artist chosen to portray this typical Renaissance scientist? What visual 'clues' has he given to tell us something about the scientist's life and work?

2. Why do you think the protestant reformers wanted to be able to read the Bible in their own language, rather than listen to it being read in Latin by a priest?

3. What effect do you think the availability of printed Bibles in different languages (like the one shown in Source 16) might have had in 16th century Europe? Would this be the same for ordinary people who could not understand Latin as for learned scholars?

Renaissance heritage

Looking back after 400 or so years, how can we sum up the Renaissance? Was it really 'a process of worldwide significance', as one 19th century historian described it? Or was it just a passing fashion, influential among wealthy and cultured upper-class families in the 15th century, but soon fading away?

As we have seen, many ordinary people in Europe, and millions more throughout the world, had little knowledge of the Renaissance while it was happening. In the centuries that followed, Renaissance tastes and ideas gradually spread round the world from their 'cradle' in 15th century Florence. How did this happen? Mainly, it came about through education. Humanist ideas proved very powerful in Europe and elsewhere in influencing education, both the methods of teaching and the subjects studied, from the 16th to the early 20th centuries. Some Renaissance ideas can be discovered in our beliefs and opinions today.

Art and achievement

As in Renaissance times, we admire individual artists and performers for their own particular achievements, in everything from rock music to architecture. We regard paintings and sculptures as beautiful objects to be admired for their own sake. Art no longer has to serve the needs of powerful princes, or the Church. This approach to art began in Renaissance times and continued for many years, as Sources 18 and 20 show.

Today, people also discuss another Renaissance idea (illustrated by the quotation in Source 19): who should pay for art, and what should its purpose be? Should works of art be purchased by wealthy individuals, to be enjoyed privately? Or should they be paid for by the state, and be displayed publicly for all to see? Do we still expect wealthy patrons to give generously to pay for beautiful buildings, paintings and statues, to benefit the community – and commemorate themselves?

'Provide then, ye princes, while ye live
That of the Muses ye befriended be
Which unto men eternity do give....'

Provide = give money; act as patrons
the Muses = ancient Greek name for the goddesses who encouraged the arts – music, painting, poetry etc.

SOURCE 19
Lines from the English poet Edmund Spenser (?1512–1599). Their message is: 'give money to encourage the arts and you will be rewarded by long-lasting fame.'

'Know then thyself, presume not God to scan,
The proper study of mankind is man.'

SOURCE 20
Lines from a poem by Alexander Pope (1688–1744).

SOURCE 18
Detail from a painting by Titian, completed c 1515. Titian's art celebrates human beauty; it does not seek to glorify princes or the Church.

RENAISSANCE HERITAGE

Using the Renaissance
The Renaissance admiration of Greek and Roman styles continued for many years. Up until the early 20th century, architects designed buildings to look like ancient temples, to make them seem bigger, stronger, or more impressive. You can see an example of one of these massive buildings in Source 21. Perhaps this admiration is not so widespread now. However, Renaissance art is still used to add 'class' or prestige to modern products (see Source 22).

Masters of the world?
The Renaissance vision of human beings as all-powerful and in control of the world has lasted almost until the present day. However, our growing awareness of the damage human beings cause to the Earth's ecology marks an important change of outlook. We are beginning to want to care for, rather than exploit, the natural world. Perhaps today we are witnessing the end of the Renaissance humanist view of men and women as 'masters of the world'?

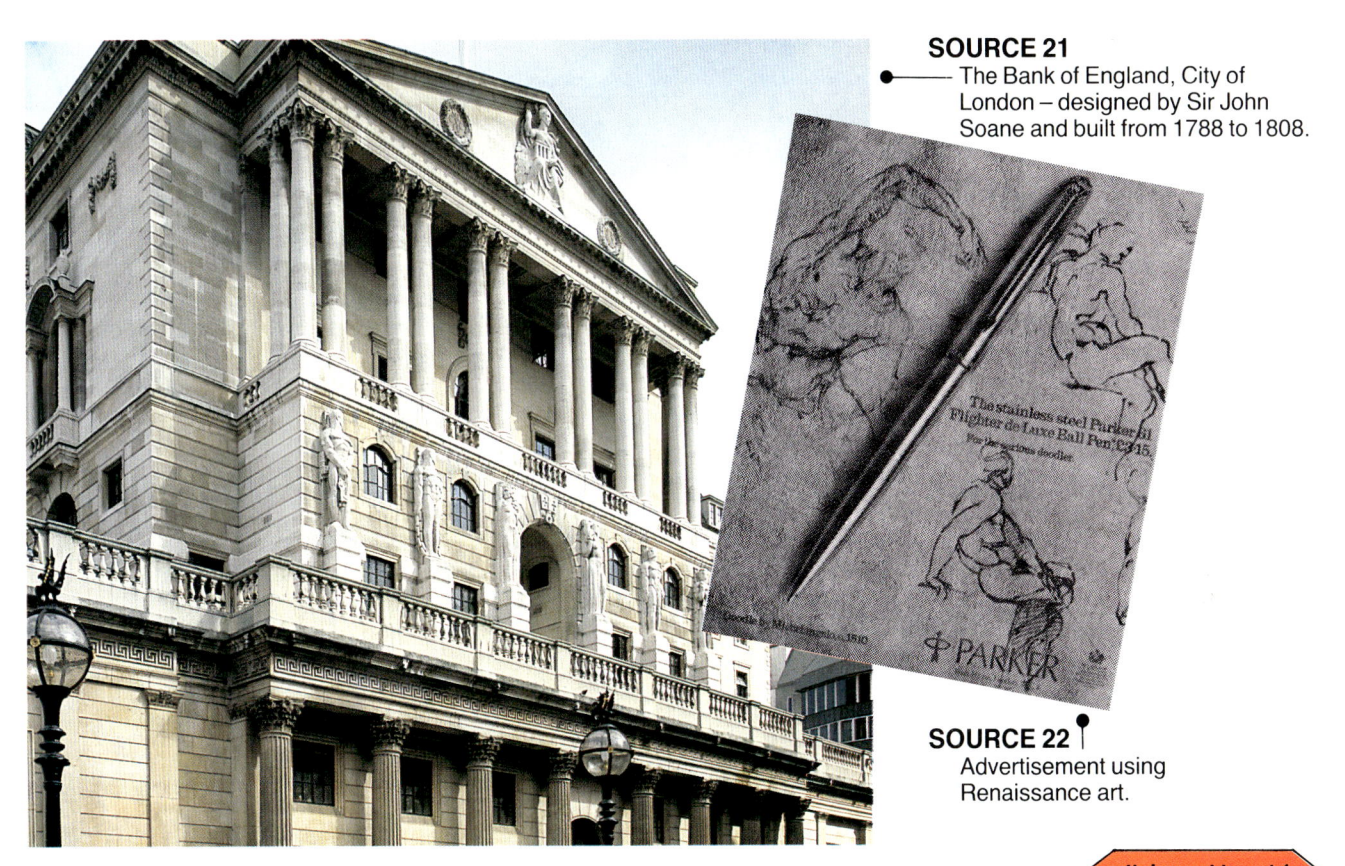

SOURCE 21
The Bank of England, City of London – designed by Sir John Soane and built from 1788 to 1808.

SOURCE 22
Advertisement using Renaissance art.

attainment target 1

1. Look back at the Sources in units 1, 2 and 3. Choose two of them to show the differences between medieval and Renaissance art *or* philosophy *or* architecture.

2. Plan a display entitled 'Life in Renaissance Italy'. What would you choose to include? Make a list of at least five items (chosen from the Sources in this book or from other reference material) that you would like to include. Now write a sentence explaining why you chose *each* of the five items.

3. Explain how each of them shows one aspect of the Renaissance.

4. In what ways do Sources 18, 19 and 20 show attitudes typical of the Renaissance?

5. Look at Source 22 on this page. Why do you think the advertisers chose to link their product with the Renaissance artist Michaelangelo?

6. What do you think that Michaelangelo himself, or other Renaissance artists, might have felt about the advertisement (Source 22) if they had been able to see it? (Pages 44–47 might help you here.)

Glossary

Academy
Place where people gather to study, hold discussions and/or display works of art.

Altarpiece
A painting designed to stand behind the altar in a Christian church.

Anatomy
The scientific study of the human body.

Ancestors
People from whom we are descended.

Astronomy
The study of space, including the stars, planets, Sun and Moon.

Bankruptcy
Financial failure (usually of a business).

Barbarian
Savage or uncivilised person.

Biased
To act or think unfairly because of strongly held opinions or beliefs.

Candidates
People hoping to be elected (chosen by vote).

Cardinal
One of the highest ranks in the Catholic Church.

Chancellor
Senior official.

Chateau (French) pronounced *sha-toe*
Originally meant 'castle'; by the 16th century, it also meant 'grand house'.

Christendom
In the 16th century, used to describe the countries of Western Europe.

Commemoration
Preserving the memory of someone or something.

Commissioned
Ordered a work of art or a building to be made, and paid for it.

Controversial
Something which people disagree about.

Courtiers
People who spent a lot of time at a ruler's court.

Cultured
Educated and knowledgeable about the arts.

Decisively
Firmly and without hesitation.

Denouncing
Strongly criticising.

Distorted
Bent or twisted out of natural shape.

Donors
People who give. In the Renaissance, donors gave works of art to churches and other public places.

Drought
Period of water shortage, when rain does not fall.

Ducal
Belonging to a duke.

Dynasty
Powerful family.

Economic depression
A time when businesses do badly, make losses or go into *bankruptcy*.

Embalmed corpse
Dead body preserved by wrapping it in cloths soaked in costly oils, herbs and spices.

Eternity
Endless time.

Extravagant
Generous and very expensive.

Formulated
Worked out and suggested as a new theory.

Fresco (means 'fresh' in Italian)
A wall-painting. The paints were spread on to a freshly plastered wall.

Friar
A man who has joined a religious organisation devoted to preaching and teaching.

Golden age
An imaginary time when everything in the world was peaceful and beautiful.

Harmony
Perfect peace. Also used to mean 'balance' and 'blending perfectly together'.

Heretic
Someone who refuses to accept the teachings (and the rules) of the Church, and follows a different set of beliefs.

Humanism
A philosophy that was very popular in *Renaissance* times. It teaches that human beings are worthy of study, respect and admiration because of their achievements.

Imitation
Copying.

Magnate
Powerful man or (rarely) woman in business.

Medieval
Belonging to the *Middle Ages*.

Memorial
Long-lasting reminder of someone's life and achievements.

Middle Ages
The period from around AD 500 to 1400.

Netherlands
In the 15th and 16th centuries, used to describe the present-day countries of Belgium and parts of northern France as well as the Netherlands itself.

Patrons
People who gave money to support artists, architects, *philosophers*, *scholars* etc.

Perspective
A way of drawing/painting to create the feeling of space and distance within a picture.

Philosophy
The seeking of wisdom and knowledge. Medieval and Renaissance philosophers studied a wide range of subjects. These included science, mathematics and human behaviour. Philosophers also discussed how human beings ought to live.

Plague
A deadly disease, carried by rats and fleas.

Pope
The leader of the Church in western Europe in *medieval* and *Renaissance* times.

Prestige
Fame, honour and respect.

Psychological
Concerned with the mind and how we think.

Realism
The artistic technique of trying to create an exact copy of the real world in a picture.

Renaissance
The revival of arts, architecture and learning, influenced by Greek and Roman designs and ideas. The Renaissance happened in Italy in the 15th century.

Role
Position or job in society.

Scholars
People who study, especially those who study at university. Used to mean people who were learned in the ancient languages (e.g. Greek and Latin) and their literature.

Showpiece
Built to display the creator's talents.

Speculation
Curiosity; deep and careful thought.

Status symbol
Something that displays its owner's wealth and power.

Sumptuous
Rich and splendid.

Symbols
Pictures or designs with a special meaning; for example, wearing school uniform 'symbolises' that you are part of the school.

Technique
The methods (e.g. painting with a brush) used by artists to produce their work.

Tormented
Unhappy and in pain.

Triumphal arch
A huge arch built during Roman times to celebrate famous victories.

Vanishing point
The 'far distance' painted within a picture using the technique of *perspective*.

Whore
Prostitute.

Pronunciation guide

Most of the people named in this book are listed here with clues on how to pronounce them.

Albrecht Dürer	Al-brekt Dure-err
Alighieri Dante	Ali-hyer-ee Dan-tey
Alessandro Botticelli	Al-eh-sand-roh Bott-ee-chell-ee
Andrea del Verrochio	An-dray-ah dell Verr-ock-ee-oh
Andrea Mantegna	An-dray-ah Man-ten-y-ah
Angelo Poliziano	An-jell-oh Poll-itz-ee-ah-noh
Aphrodite	Afro-die-tee
Azzo Visconti	Atzo Vis-con-tee
Bartolommeo Dei	Bar-toll-om-may-oh Day-ee
Bartolommeo Scala	Bar-toll-om-may-oh Skar-lah
Battista Sforza	Bat-tees-tah Sfortz-ah
Benozzo Gozzoli	Ben-otz-zoh Gotz-oh-lee
Bertaldo di Giovanni	Bert-al-doh dee Gee-oh-van-ee
Cervantes	Cerr-van-tays/Therr-van-tays
Chiostro degli Aranci	Kee-os-troh delly Ar-an-chee
Ciriaco d'Ancona	Syr-ee-ack-oh Dan-coh-nah
Cosimo de' Medici	Cos-ee-moh deh Med-ee-chee
Diane de Poitiers	Dee-ahn der Pwat-ee-ay
Don Quixote	Don Kee-ho-tay
Donato Bramante	Don-ah-toh Bram-an-tay
Domenico da Cortona	Dom-ay-nee-koh dah Core-toh-nah
Federico da Montefeltro	Fed-er-ee-ko dah Mon-tay-fell-troh
Ferrante	Ferr-ant-tay
Filippo Brunelleschi	Philleep-oh Brew-nell-ess-key
Francesco Petrarch	Fran-chess-koh Pet-rark
Francesco Ubertini	Fran-chess-koh Yew-ber-tee-nee
Galileo Galilei	Gal-ee-lay-oh Gal-ee-lay-ee
Giorgio Vasari	Gee-or-gee-oh Vas-ar-ee
Giovanna Cenami	Gee-oh-van-nah Chen-ah-mee
Giovanni Arnolfini	Gee-oh-van-ee Arnol-fee-nee
Giovanni Bellini	Gee-oh-van-ee Bell-ee-nee
Giovanni Rucellai	Gee-oh-van-nee Roo-chell-ay
Girolamo Savonarola	Gee-roh-lah-moh Sav-on-ah-row-lah
Hernan Cortes	Hair-nan Kor-tay-z
Isabella d'Este	Ees-ah-bell-ah Destay
Jacob Zech	Yah-kob Zeckh
Leon Battista Alberti	Lay-on Bat-tist-ah Al-ber-tee
Leonardo da Vinci	Lay-on-ard-oh dah Vin-chee
Lippo Memmi	Lee-poh Mem-mee
Lorenzo Ghiberti	Lor-ent-zoh Jib-air-tee
Luca Pacioli	Loo-kah Pah-chee-oh-lee
Lucrezia Borgia	Loo-cretz-ee-ah Bore-jah
Marsilio Ficino	Mar-sill-ee-oh Fich-ee-noh
Martin Vaquez de Arce	Mar-teen Va-kess deh Ar-say
Michaelangelo Buonarotti	Mee-kell-an-jell-oh Bew-on-ah-rot-ee
Michelozzo de Bartolommeo	Mee-kell-otz-zoh deh Bar-toll-om-ay-oh
Niccolò Machiavelli	Nick-ol-oh Mack-ee-ah-velly
Paulo Uccello	Pow-lo Yew-chell-o
Pico della Mirandola	Pee-coh dell-ah Mir-an-doh-lah
Pier Paulo Vergerio	Pee-air Pow-loh Vair-gair-ee-oh
Pierre de Ronsard	Pee-air der Ron-sar
Platina	Plat-ee-nah
Raphael	Raf-ay-ell
Rogier van der Weyden	Rodj-ee-ay van derr Vay-den
Scamozzi	Scam-otz-zee
Sebastian de Almonacid	Seb-ass-tee-anne deh All-mon-ah-seed
Simone Martini	See-moh-nay Mar-tee-nee
'Titian'	Tish-anne
Tomasso Masaccio	Tom-ah-soh Maz-arch-ee-oh
Tycho Brahe	Tie-koh Bra-hay

Index

Page numbers in **bold** refer to illustrations/captions

Alberti, Leon Battista **36**, **40**, 46, 62
Aphrodite **38**
architecture 10, 18, 21, 23, 34, 36-37, 46, 51-52, 59
art 14-16, 24-25, 28-31, 43, 55, 58
artistic techniques 15, 29-31, 45, 50, 55
astronomy 45, 48-9, 60

Bandinelli, Baccio **42**
Bank of England **59**
bankers 7, **10-11**
Baptistery, Florence **21**
beauty 38-39
Bellini, Giovanni **16**, **32**, 45, 62
Bible **57**
books **5**, **15**, **17**, **56**
Borgia, Lucrezia **39**, 62
Botticelli, Alessandro 5, **25**, **38**, 45, 62
Brahe, Tycho **48**, 62
Bramante, Donato 46, 62
Brunelleschi, Filippo 5, **21**, 46-47, 62

cardinals 12-13, 60
Cathedral, Florence **3**, 5, **21**, 44, 46, **47**
Cervantes 53, 62
Chambord, Chateau **5**, **52**
China 4, 8, 10
Church 10, 12-13, 15, 20, 27, 40, 49, 57
  government 13
cities 8-10, 20-21
city-states **4**, 6, 16-18
clock **56**
Columbus, Christopher **5**, 48, 53
Constance, Council 4, **13**
Cortes, Hernan **49**, 62
'cradle of the Renaissance' 22-23
craft guilds 9
craft workers 7-9, 43

d'Ancona, Ciriaco **34**, 62
Dante, Alighieri 14-15, 62
defence 16-17
d'Este, Isabella **19**, 62
discovery 46-47
Doge of Venice **16**
Donatello 25, 44
Durër, Albrecht **50**, 62

education 58
Erasmus 51, **57**
Eyck, Jan van 5, **50**

financial families 10-11
Florence 4-5, **6-7**, 10, **17**, **20-24**, **26-29**, 44-46, **48**
France **4**, 6, 51-52, **54**
frescos **29-30**

Galileo **49**, 62
Genoa 4, 6, 8-9
Germany 4, 50-51
Ghiberti, Lorenzo **21**, 62
Ghirlandaio, Domenico **26**
Gozzoli, Benozzo **23**, **43**, 62
Greece 4, 6, 34

Henry, Prince, the Navigator 48
history, learning from 36-37
houses 11, **18**, **36-37**
Humanism 3, 4, 40-44, 51, 53, 58, 60

investment company **11**
Italy 3-**4**, 6-9, 16-17, 22, 54

jewellery 11, **53**

learning 14-15, 42-43
Luther, Martin, 5, **57**

Machiavelli, Niccolò **17**, **37**, 62
Mantegna, Andrea **13**, **35**, 62
Mantua **13**, **36**
maps **48**
Martellus, Henricus **48**
Martini, Simone **14-15**, 62
Masaccio, Tomasso **29**, 44, 62
medieval art 30
Medici family 10-11, **22-24**, **39**
Medici, Cosimo de' **22-23**, 62
Medici, Lorenzo de' **5**, **24**-25, 45
Memmi, Lippo **14-15**, 62
merchants 7-**8**, 10-11, 20-21
Michaelangelo Buonarotti 5, 40-**41**, 43-**46**, **54-55**, 62
Michelozzo de Bartolommeo 10, **23**
Milan 4, 10-11, 18, 46
'Mona Lisa' **5**, **41**
money 10
Montacute House, Somerset **51**
Montefeltro, Federico da **18-19**, **42**, 62

natural world 32-33
Netherlands 4, **6**, **28**-29, 50, 60

Pacioli, Luca **56**, 62
Pantheon 46
Parthenon, Athens **36**
patrons 3, 16-19, 52

perspective **31**, 33
Petrarch, Francesco **35**, 62
Pico della Mirandola, Giovanni **46**, 62
Piero della Francesco 18, **31**
poets 51, **53**, **58**
Poitiers, Diane de **52-53**, 62
Popes **12-13**, 24, 61
Portinari family **28**
princes 16-19
printing 5, 42, 56-57

Raphael **33**, 62
realism 29-31, 33, 61
Reformation 56-57
rinascati 28
Rome 4, 12-13, 34, 41, 45
Rucellai, Giovanni **20**-21, 62

Savonarola, Friar Girolamo **26-27**, 62
Scala, Bartolommeo **22**, 62
Scamozzi **36-37**, 62
science 46-47, 56
sculpture **21**, **24-25**, **38**, **43**, **54-55**
Sforza, Battista **18**-19, 41, 62
Shakespeare, William **5**, 51
Siena 4, 15, **26**
silks 9
Sistine Chapel, Rome 5, **41**, 45, **54**
Sixtus IV, Pope 24
slaves 9
solar systems **49**
Spain 4, 6, 52-53
spices 9

temple, Greek **36**
textile workers 9
'Titian' **43**, **44-45**, **58**, 62
towns **6-7**
trade 7-9, 16-18
Turkey 6
Tuscany **4**, **6-7**

Ubertini, Francesco **20**, 62
Uccello, Paolo **17**, 62
universe 48-49
Urbino 4, 6, **18**

Vasari, Giorgio **20**, 28-29, 62
Vecellio, Tiziano *see* 'Titian'
Venice 4, 6-7, **8-9**, **16**, 44-45
Verrochio, Andrea del 5, **25**, 62
Vinci, Leonardo da 5, **19**, **32-33**, **40-41**, **45-47**, 52, 62
Visconti, Azzo **18-19**, 62

wars 17

© CollinsEducational, an imprint of HarperCollins*Publishers*

Fiona Macdonald asserts the moral right to be identified as the author of this work.

All rights reserved. No part of this publication may be reproduced, stored in a retrieval system, or transmitted in any form or by any means, electronic, mechanical, photocopying, recording or otherwise, without the prior permission of the publisher.

First published 1992 by CollinsEducational
77-85 Fulham Palace Road
Hammersmith
London W6 8JB

ISBN 0 00 327242 7

Cover design by Glynis Edwards
Book designed by Don Parry, Peartree Design Associates
Series planned by Nicole Lagneau
Edited by Stephen Attmore
Picture research by Celia Dearing
Artwork by Peter Dennis, Linda Rogers Associates pages 4-5, 47, 49 and Don Parry, Peartree Design Associates, pages 11, 31
Production by Mandy Inness

Typeset by Dorchester Typesetting Group Ltd

Printed and bound by Stige-Arti Grafiche, Italy

Acknowledgements

The author would like to thank Stephen Attmore, who edited this book, for his patience and encouragement. The book has benefited greatly from his comments and suggestions.

Every effort has been made to contact the holders of copyright material but if any have been inadvertently overlooked the publishers will be pleased to make the necessary arrangements at the first opportunity.

Photographs The publishers would like to thank the following for permission to reproduce photographs on these pages:

T = top, B = bottom, R = right, C = centre, L = left

Alinari 22; Bibliothéque Nationale, Paris 39, 52B; Biblioteca Medicea Laurenziana/D. Pineider 56BL; The Bodleian Library, Oxford 8T (Ms Bodl.264 f.219r), 30T (Ms Laud.Misc.409 f.3v); F. Bird 13T, 21R; The Bridgeman Art Library/Uffizi, Florence 14, 18TL & TR, 25B, 28, 38B, Palazzo Ducale, Mantua 13B, Fabbri 21L, 23B, 24, 38T, 54L, 56T, Palazzo Medici-Riccardi, Florence 23T, San Marco dell' Angelico, Florence 26T, 27, S. Trinita, Florence 26B, Galleria della Marche, Urbino 31T, Accademia, Venice 40, Vatican Museums 41T, Lauros-Giraudon 47, Prado, Madrid 50L; By Permission of the British Library 6R (Ms Add.24098 f.29v), 9 (Ms Add.15277 f.16r), 10T (Ms 27695 f.8r), 12, 15 (Ms Sloane 4016 f.30), 17B (Ms Y.T.36 f.145), 34R (Ms Facs. 72. 11), 48B (Add. 15760 f.68v-69r), 56BR, 57; Reproduced by Courtesy of the Trustees of the British Museum 46, 33; C.M. Dixon 48T; Giraudon/Palais Royal, Turin 45; Robert Harding Picture Library 3, 34L, 36L, 52T; Instituto Nazionale per la Grafica, Rome 42T; Louvre/© photo R.M.N. 19, 41B; The Mansell Collection 35; © MAS 53T; Reproduced by Courtesy of the Trustees of the National Gallery, London 17T, 32B, 50R; Courtesy Parker Pen UK Ltd 59R; Preussischer Kulturebesitz/Staatliche Museum 44; Rijksmuseum 20; Scala 18B, 36R, Palazzo Vechio, Florence 7, Vatican Museums 8B, 54R, Accademia, Venice 16, Bargello, Florence 25T, S. Maria Novella, Florence 29, Badia, Florence 30B, Galleria Nazionale, Urbino 42B, Or San Michele, Florence, 43T, Palazzo Medici-Riccardi, Florence 43B, Castello Sforzesco, Milan 55, Galleria Borghese, Rome 58; Society of Antiquaries, London 56C; Courtesy of the Board of Trustees of the V. & A. 53B; Windsor Castle, Royal Library © 1991 Her Majesty The Queen 32; Tim Woodcock 51, 59L; Zefa 6L.

Cover photograph: Robert Harding

The author and publishers gratefully acknowledge the following publications from which written sources in this book are drawn:

The Fifteenth Century: The Prospect of Europe by Margaret Aston, 1968, and *Cities of Destiny* by J R Hale, 1968, published by Thames & Hudson; *The Renaissance* by A Brown, 1968, published by Longman Group Ltd; *The Story of Art* by E Gombrich, 1960, published by Phaidon Press; Penguin Books Ltd for extracts from: *Penguin Dictionary of Quotations*, 1960, *The Prince* by Niccolò Machiavelli (edited and translated by George Bull, Penguin Classics, 1961), *Early Renaissance* by M Levey (Pelican), 1967; Facts on File, USA for extract from the introduction to *The Encyclopedia of the Renaissance*, T Bergin & J Speake (eds), published by Batsford (B T) Ltd 1987; *Culture and Society in Italy 1290-1420* by J Larner, 1970, Batsford (B T) Ltd; Macmillan Publishers Ltd for extract from *Patrons and Artists in the Italian Renaissance*, D S Chambers (ed), 1970; Cambridge University Press for quote from *The Renaissance* by R M Letts; extracts from *Annalists and Historians* by D Hay, 1977 and from *Medieval People* by Eileen Power; Peter Burke for extracts from *The Civilisation of the Renaissance in Italy* by J Burckhardt, 1990.